# Keep Your Sexy Sacred

## WINNING THE WAR BETWEEN THE FLESH AND THE SPIRIT

## SABRINA UNIVERSAL LAWTON

# Contents

Beth & Blake,

Thank you for your time, lovely energy, and intention! You are a power couple! Here's to much love and prosperity!

May this book "KISS" your soul.

Universal Love,
Suzy

P.S. Grateful for our connection 💋

# Acknowledgements

I dedicate this book in loving memory of my late Uncle Bruce, a man who may have had "less than" by man's standards, but was rich in the spirit, for he was love. He was my earthly father figure, the first man who ever loved me for me. He was also a father to many others, namely his three amazing children, Brittney, Bianca, and Brandon. Just as you always reminded us, I will "*stay focused,*" Uncle Bruce.

On your day of passing, you left for me inside your wallet one of the few childhood photos I have. On the back of the old, wallet-sized photo was written, "still love her." Your spirit knew that in order for me to complete this body of work, I would need to reacquaint myself with the innocent child inside me who did nothing wrong. For the first time, I saw my younger self in the beauty, love, and light in which you saw me. I love you. Thank you for always speaking life into me. May you laugh, sing, and dance in all eternity.

To my husband Eric, the love of my life. I am eternally grateful to spend my life with you. What often feels like paradise *is* our life together. We are living the *Kingdom of Heaven* in our midst! I am honored that you are my sacred soul partner, my earth angel, and my protector. Thank you for walking with me through the fire on the way to getting here! You have my loyalty forever and a day. May your joy be full, and your rewards be sevenfold! I am grateful for our covenant of love under God, since before our wedding day on 07/07/07 to eternity. I love you.

To my handsome son, Martin. I am grateful to be your mother. You are a powerful force of divine love. Your kind, loving nature and spiritual intelligence are beyond your years. I know your path was not always easy. Thank you for forgiving me for the role I played in the cause of your pain. You have already had so many spiritual conquests and you've only just begun. My prayer is that you would see yourself the way God see's you. A gentle giant— God's Kingdom awaits you. Thank you for saying yes to God; you've already won.

To my beautiful daughter, Savannah. You are a star! A divinely created gift from God. Thank you for comforting me when I was crying one morning about how hard it was for me to keep going in this work I had not yet fully known. You rolled your innocent five-year-old eyes, shook your head, and sighed as you grabbed a paper and pencil and began to doodle. You handed me the paper and to my surprise, it read: Evolve to Love Mom. The words were graced by a big, beautiful flower in the center of the drawing. You inspire me to keep going no matter what!

Thank you to my grandmother for being a loving presence in my life and for being the first to introduce me to God when I was a child. Thank you to my mother and father for bringing me into this world. You provided me with the genetic coding and life experiences I would need to carry out my mission to help the world conquer the silent killer in most of our lives: spiritual warfare.

To my entire family, I love you. I thank you for your role in the story of my life. If my story offends anyone in any way, I ask your forgiveness. I couldn't risk not answering God's calling at the expense of your comfort. I did not use the actual names of many people in my story, because my story isn't about their sin. It's about my own sin. More importantly, it's about my ability to transcend it by walking in the spirit. I pray you have peace in understanding that my story is for God's glory. I pray you rejoice over every life it saves.

Thank you, David Hancock and the Morgan James Publishing family for helping me to birth "KYSS" throughout the earth! A labor of love, and beautiful child of God indeed. Thank you,

Michelle Kulp, and Sadaf Karimi, for sharing your compelling stories herein with our readers.

Thank you to my business mentor, Tasha Chen. This book would not be written had I not traveled along your path. Thank you, Dr. Timothy Owens Moore, the wild card who the Holy Spirit dropped into my laptop, straight from the *universe,* through the *world-wide-web*! I never knew you a single day in my life until after viewing a few of your lectures online. I felt a deep spiritual prompting to reach out to you, and as act of obedience, I did. Your response to reading my manuscript helped me to believe in the power of my story to heal others if I just had the courage to share it.

I am eternally grateful to God, Jesus, the Holy Spirit within me, the Spirit in the plant medicine, and the many earth angels, now in Heaven, who fought the good fight for love. You have helped me conquer fear with faith. You have shown me love and grace. I dedicate my life to you.

*"I can do all things through Christ who gives me strength." ~Philippians 4:1 ESV*

# An Interview with the Love of My Life

**Wonder of Women. WonderNews. by Claudia Parker**

1. **Please write your name as you wish it to appear in the publication?** Eric

2. **What was it about Sabrina that first drew you in?** It was my wife's understanding that each of us are spiritual beings having a human experience. When my wife and I met, I had recently returned from war in Iraq with the US Army. I was not in connection with my spirit, nor my emotions, and moved through life in very human form, fulfilling needs of survival and desire, with an enormous hole in my heart and a disconnect from God. Despite my shortcomings, my wife introduced me to what it means to be a spiritual being and live for a greater purpose other than self. She fed me spiritually and emotionally, which was something I had never experienced before.

3. **As her husband, how did it make you feel when you learned about the emotional and physical trauma she's endured?** Initially I carried mixed emotions, mostly consisting of empathy, sadness, and anger. It hurt to know that an innocent child could endure such pain and sorrow. My wife taught me the meaning of power in your pain and expanded my understanding of the spiritual journey we each experience. She taught me that her story was not quite as unique as I had imaged, and that the majority suffer from a past riddled with mental, physical, and sexual trauma. I learned that the power to utilize our stories to define our

purpose is a gift from God that can be tapped into, given the correct guidance.

4. **Many marriages have trouble and have experienced infidelity; it's easy to leave. But what was it about your wife that made you stay?** My wife helped me to realize that we are much greater than our actions. We both realized that what we were experiencing were common challenges in marriage, and that God would bless our relationship if we could see beyond the storm we were in. We focused on addressing the concerns that got us to that point in our relationship and gave our relationship to God to nurture.

5. **How does it make you feel to see Sabrina using her pain as a passion to help others?** Her ability to transmute the pain from her past never ceases to amaze me. My wife's ability to utilize her God-gifted talents for the betterment of all sometimes comes with a heavy weight attached to it. She has dedicated her life to the selfless service of others, and her light shines with a pure brightness. She understands that this can sometimes be a thankless job and does not seek gratitude in return for her work. I have seen life-changing results in quick reply, in many of those who have been blessed to work with her.

6. **What advice would you give other men about the process of healing their relationship?** Invest in your relationship with God and continue to grow spiritually, both as a couple and individually. Our best self is ever-evolving and a work in progress. Become best friends and create time together to just "be." Plan your journey together as a couple, defining a destination and manifesting your dreams through visualization and prayer.

# Introduction

No matter where you are in our world—from India to America, Africa to Korea, and places in between—sexuality, spirituality, and the role of women are widely misunderstood. Globally we are suffering a moral and spiritual deficit, largely due to overly masculinized societies. The feminine characteristics of God are being forgotten and women are being reduced to objects of visual pleasure and physical stimuli, not worthy to stand on the pulpits of many prominent religions to this day.

*Keep Your Sexy Sacred* has been written to activate the Divine Power within women and guide men to understanding that women are their missing link to God. God is described in our biblical texts as both *Male* and *Female*, and even more so as *Spirit and Love.* Perhaps unintentionally, religion has created a God who is very masculine in nature. The consequence is that women are worshiping men as if they were God, while men remain deeply disconnected from the feminine nature of God within themselves and women. Both suffer in silence.

We are on the precipice of a spiritual breakdown—or a spiritual breakthrough. We now have a critical choice to make regarding whether we evolve or devolve as a human race. To collectively evolve, we must restore the balance of power between the masculine and feminine energies in our world. This is the way to love. I will begin the paradigm shift by referring to God using the feminine terms "SHe" and "HEr" as often as I am inspired.

When God said, *"let **us** make humans in our image and likeness"* I am pretty sure God wasn't talking to a bunch of masculine spirits. I have believed God is both feminine and masculine for some time; however, I first *experienced* the feminine presence of God after ingesting a plant medicine called Ayahuasca. "Aya," for short, is a brew consisting of just two organic plants used in traditional spiritual ceremonies among the indigenous peoples of the Amazon basin. I want to point out that I had been seeking, finding, and sharing the love of God through my organization Evolve To Love® for a number of years prior to ingesting this plant medicine.

*"Every moving thing that liveth shall be meat for you; even as the green herb have I given you all things." ~Genesis: 9-3 KJV*

With regard to my personal walk with God, this medicine was the very thing that would deepen my relationship and catapult me into the next chapter of my life. There were so many defining moments for me that I have dedicated an entire chapter to the power of plant medicines. I share specific examples of how they have helped me and many others obtain relief from chronic physical disease, and surprisingly, gain a new way of understanding God. Before we seek to understand plants, let's seek to understand Woman and her true role in all creation.

Does not the word "*he*" increase when it marries the letter "*s*" to spell the word "*she*"? Is not the word "man" more abundant when joined with the two letters "wo," spelling the word "*woman*"? And likewise, woman cannot fully actualize herself without understanding her own masculinity, or the male within the "*fe*"-male. The complete harmony between two seemingly separate beings is exactly what God had in mind when we were created. To any man who thinks it is balanced as it is, balance is never achieved when one side of the scale does not agree. Many would agree that there is great disparity.

*"This explains why a man leaves his father and mother
and is joined to his wife, and the two are united into one."
~Genesis 2:24 NLT*

While I am of no religious affiliation, I do believe in and follow the wisdom teachings of the Bible, which I have affectionately given the acronym "Basic Instructions Before Leaving Earth." I will be referencing the *Universal Laws of Love* herein frequently as they are the foundation upon which my points stand. I prepare you in advance: the God and Jesus or *Yaweh and Yeshua* this book will introduce you to are likely very different from what your religion has taught you.

This book is not intended to lead you to, or away from, any particular religion. It does serve to give you a new pathway to God. It is true—there is nothing new under the sun. It's the way we look at things that changes what we see. God is Love. The problem, as proven by the condition of many of our private, and thanks to social media, very public lives, is that we do not know what love is.

To solve this macro problem, we will begin at the micro level. We will begin with you. The condition of your life is the byproduct of your family tree, your childhood experiences, your most intimate relationships, and the environment surrounding you. What were the messages you received about God and sex? What were your actual experiences? Your programming around these two topics is in direct proportion to whether you primarily experience peace, love, and joy, or anger, fear, and sadness. Who are you really? You will discover who you are when you *unlearn* who you were taught to be.

*"Jesus answered them, "Is it not written in your Law, 'I said,
you are gods'?" ~John 10:34 ESV*

Are you willing to believe what Jesus, the Great Teacher of Love has stated? You are a god. Whether or not this statement makes you comfortable is a tell-tale sign regarding whether you are merely practicing religious rituals or in a personal relationship with God.

This journey is not for the faint of heart. You can expect that whatever does not serve your soul will rise to the surface. As with any detox, the purging does not always feel good. Whatever comes up, embrace the idea that you must *feel it to heal it.*

Read this book cover to cover. Do not attempt to rummage through the fruit basket, picking out of it only what you think you need. You are the farmer of your life. Journey through the process of weeding, pruning, sowing, cutting down, seeding, watering, bearing, and reaping your harvest. Only by your labor of love will you truly appreciate and enjoy your good fruit.

Take this opportunity to become new. Do not be afraid to die to old thoughts, beliefs, and patterns of behavior that have kept you captive to the woes and wounds of the flesh.

*"O death, where is your victory?*
*O death, where is your sting?"*
*~1 Corinthians 15:55 ESV*

I have walked through the valleys and the shadows of death. I have transcended the dark nights of the soul. I have died to my old self. I rise again in grace, truth, and love. Here I stand, wearing the full armor of God, shouting from the mountain top: *fear no evil.* Not the evil done unto you, not the evil you have done, not even the evil you imagine possible. Trust that when you decide to deal with the afflictions of the flesh, HEr grace will see you through.

## My "Why" for writing KYSS:

I have endured, unleashed, and healed from a multitude of sins:

- **I was born to a teenage mother.**
- **My father was incarcerated for rape.**
- **I suffered a violent near-death experience.**
- **I was molested at age five.**
- **I was first introduced to porn at age seven.**
- **Masturbation became my escape.**
- **I experienced adversity due to my race.**
- **I have suffered from depression.**
- **I was under-educated by man's standards.**
- **I have committed adultery.**
- **I have been divorced.**
- **I am healed by the power of God's Love.**

It was when I began to study the *Universal Laws of Love* as written in the Great Book of Life, and other sacred texts, that I realized *"all things were working together for my good" (Romans 8:28)*. In order for me to show you how to turn from the flesh, I had to have known what it was like to walk in the flesh. In order for me to show you how to *Keep Your Sexy Sacred*, I had to have experienced what it was like when my sexy was not sacred. Wouldn't you rather seek advice from someone who has both experienced and transcended your pain? Those with experience are among the best teachers.

After a series of painful, gut-wrenching, and life-threatening experiences, I surrendered my ego identity and allowed God to run the show. I ended my lucrative, sixteen-year career in corporate leadership and created Evolve To Love®, a Spiritual Advising organization founded on the principle that *"Every Problem has a Spiritual Solution®."*

I am blissfully married to the love my life. God is the center of our love. Among many other amazing experiences, we regularly have awesome, sexy, s*acred* sex! We are parents to two beautiful children. We are love, we are joy, we are peace, we are health, and we are grateful to experience the simple abundance and true wealth of God. Yes, I know it is not good to boast, but … as the scriptures say, "If you want to boast, boast only about the LORD" (1 Corinthians 1:31). I am answering God's calling on my life and sharing the "how" with you. Your reward for following along with me is the experience of the Kingdom of Heaven in your midst. There is but one caveat: you have free will—your participation in your healing is required.

You are reading *KYSS* because you have answered God's calling to partake of HEr nourishing spiritual food. It does not matter whether you are young or old, rich or poor, white or black, female or male, religious or agnostic, gay or straight. This book transcends these dimensions of density and speaks to you in the space where we are all *One Universal* S*pirit.* Upon embodying these *Universal Laws of Love*, you can expect to see life through new lenses, and with 20/20 vision.

With your enhanced Spiritual IQ®, you will attract relationships rooted in fertile ground. You will water the parts of your life that have been dried up by guilt, shame, lack of forgiveness, and pain. You will bear the good fruit God intends for you.

This is the cost of **truth**: You will no longer see what never was, nor hear what makes no sound. Is it a sacrifice to release illusions and receive the peace of God?

Do not delay in embracing the idea that by simply agreeing to reexamine everything you've been taught about God and sex, you *will win* the war between the flesh and the spirit! The rest of your blessed life depends on it.

# PART 1: THE FLESH WAR

*"The best way to solve problems and to fight against war is through dialogue."* ~Malala Yousafzai

# Chapter 1: Born in Sin

*"Behold, I was brought forth in iniquity, and in sin did my mother conceive me." ~Psalm 51:5 ESV*

Let's not get judgmental about what it means to be born in sin. When we judge things, we miss the point and the moral of the story. There may be many things in this book you are tempted to judge. Do not fall into judgment or you will miss your love lesson. Perceptions are often deceptions. If the role of Jesus was to save us from sin by teaching us the power of love, then it would make perfect sense that he would be born in perceived "sin," considering he was conceived by a woman who lived with a man who was not Jesus's biological father. We know his father was not of flesh but was the very Spirit of God. Jesus is the perfect example of how one can rise above ridicule, judgement, and despondency.

One very good biblical example of the fallacy of judgment and false accusation was when Jesus cast out a mute demon from a man. When the demon had left, the man could speak. Some people accused Jesus of casting out demons using the power of the demon Beelzebub (another name for Satan).

*"Jesus knew their thoughts and said to them: 'Any kingdom divided against itself will be ruined, and a house divided against itself will fall.'" ~Luke 11:17 NIV*

Everyone has a story. I have a story. You have a story. Because you were born of this world, I am certain that woven into the fabric of your story is pain. Your pain was likely caused by someone else's sin, which is, by definition, a transgression against Universal Law.

The energetic shift you need to disrupt former patterns of pain can only come by way of a *spiritual solution*. Your personal walk with God is the only light you need to shine away the darkness. Religious laws and flaws have not done well to govern us. If your religious congregation's ministry stretches far beyond the laws of man and reaches deep into the universal wisdom and understanding our Loving God has to offer, you are in a safe place. If fear, judgement, condemnation, guilt, shame, and lack of faith are still with you, I suggest you take this opportunity to do some observation without condemnation.

*"But now we have been released from the law, for we died to it and are no longer captive to its power. Now we can serve God, not in the old way of obeying the letter of the law, but in the new way of living in the Spirit."* ~Romans 7:6 NLT

You have been born in a world that quickly caused you to forget who you are. Take the often painful, yet liberating journey to remembering that you are spirit. In this life, we all experience dark nights of the soul on our way to the proverbial mountain top. The battle is hell, but the winning is heavenly!

This is "The Game of Life," "The Matrix," "The Hunger Games," "The Wakanda Forever"—we are fighting the good fight to win! You are God's very own personal Avatar. This world of vibrant colors, mountainous peaks, glorious terrain, and creatures of every kind is a beautiful garden created for *Love* to experience all its *Majesty* through you and me. The keys to connecting with our Creator are hidden within plain sight, in all of nature.

This is a true story about your ability to evolve from nothing, no one, and nowhere to something, someone, and now here. The time is now to reexamine the roots of your existence, beyond your sexuality, religion, race, trauma, pain, insecurities, and ego. The very attainable goal is that you would fix your attention on the love which you are. When you do, all that is love will find you.

As you read on, be open, be present, be still, and breathe deeply. Inhale the new life God is offering you. Exhale what no longer serves you. Keep *KYSS* on your night stand, or in another sacred space in your home. Give yourself complete permission to plant within your heart these carefully crafted seeds which have been sown with *Divine Intervention*. Water them in the garden of your life and you will have no choice but to bear good fruit and be the reflection of God's light.

*"No one lights a lamp and then puts it under a basket. Instead, a lamp is placed on a stand, where it gives light to everyone in the house." ~Matthew 5:15 NLT*

## Alive and in the Flesh

I, Sabrina Universal Lawton, chose to reflect the physical projection of an African-American female. I was born in Los Angeles, California in 1977. America was on the heels of the civil rights movement. While the Emancipation Proclamation was issued in 1863, it would be roughly a century later before *everyone* would begin exploring true freedom and justice for all. This is still a work in progress throughout our world today.

I was conceived by a sixteen-year-old teen mother, and my father was a pedophile and drug addict. He spent most of his life in prison, and is now serving a life sentence for his crimes. The rape of a minor was his first offense. Allegedly he had sex with his then girlfriend's thirteen-year-old daughter. My mom informed me that his response to the accusation was that she was "fast," a slang word referring to a girl acting older than she actually is. The law would favor the young girl, landing my father in prison for the first of his California three strikes.

In my early formative years, I lived with my grandmother, a devout Jehovah's Witness, and my grandfather, who passed away when I was in my teens. My grandfather was an authoritative, Christian-identified businessman, who worked hard to provide a roof over our heads and food on the table. My grandfather impregnated my grandmother when she was in her early teens. He was at least a decade older, with a wife and multiple children of his own at the time.

Unfortunately, the startling age difference between man and wife was not uncommon in those days, especially in the African-American community where during times of slavery, many women were sexually objectified and victims of rape—often prior to having their first menstruations or other rites of passage into womanhood. Regardless of your race, religion, or country of origin, I have a knowing from a space deep within my soul that our stories, our family dynamics, and our cultural challenges are more similar than they are different.

My grandfather eventually divorced his former wife and wed my grandmother. Together, they had seven children. True to her religion, along with many other women of that time, my grandmother often sacrificed her opinions to his authority. She kept the house in order, cooked, cleaned, and served my grandfather his dinner most evenings. Whenever my grandfather was home, we'd find him relaxing on his oversized chaise in the formal living room. Keeping him company was the TV and a big, green bottle of J&B Scotch.

No one was allowed to play around in the formal living room. Those were his special quarters for winding down. I tended to think the liquor actually wound him up. On the one hand, he was a comical, passionate man who loved his family. On the other, he could be short-tempered, agitated, and bitter with alcohol and unfulfilled dreams.

My grandmother was a kind, loving, and gentle woman. She regularly studied the Jehovah's Witness Bible, Watch Tower, and Awake magazines with her children and grandchildren. I found it fascinating how vibrant the colors of the people, animals, trees, and nature scenes were. These images were to reflect the people of the "New Order" as the Jehovah's Witnesses put it. As is customary with her religion, we went to meetings and door-to-door field services. While I do not subscribe to her religion, it put me at ease as a child to feel the love of the God of her understanding.

Regardless of how many religions have inadvertently transferred the vibration of fear over love, and judgment over non-judgment, the intention of most who subscribe to religion is to draw nearer to God. And God is so good that SHe will meet you wherever you seek HEr. In my innocence, I could feel the intention behind my grandmother's devotion to her religion. As I became an adult, I began to realize that man-made rules and misinterpretations of scripture have often created a disconnect between intention and actual embodiment of God.

Of all seven children, the first to be baptized was my mother. She was just thirteen years old. The perception that we were a middle-class, *Jehovah*-fearing family was extremely important to uphold. That image was abruptly shattered with my conception. My grandparents quickly tried to right my mother's wrong by having her get married.

As you could imagine, my biological father was not available at the time, so she decided on a young man named Virgil. He was abusive and would frequently have violent, angry outbursts towards my mother. Just days after a frantic call to her parents, when a desperate plea for her return home was denied, Virgil shook my three-month-young infant body violently, before delivering a crushing blow to my delicate, not fully hardened skull.

I was rushed to the hospital for stitches in the shape of a large horseshoe on the top, left side of my head. I can still feel the scarring through my thick, natural hair to this day. It is astonishing how certain memories stick with you. While I was only three months old when it happened, I have had occasional flashes throughout my life of being rolled down a long hallway on what I now know to be a hospital gurney, while gazing up at a row of lights in the halls of the ICU.

The memory of my experience was not what bothered me. It was the *energy* of my experience that would remain for what felt like an excruciatingly painful lifetime. That day marked the moment when the fear of death was deposited into my being. It would take me almost two decades to recognize that this one defining moment was the root cause for why I lived my life in a constant state of fear. As stated best by Spiritual Thought Leader Panache Desai, emotion is *energy in motion*. Imagine the emotional energies of fear, anger, shock, and sadness, which swirled and festered around my young baby body as a consequence of this event.

## Hello Fear

Fear causes you to hold your breath, so as not to *feel*, and open your eyes wide as a deer in headlights—in disbelief of what has happened or what is to come. Fear accelerates your heart rate as your fight-or-flee instincts set in. Fear will paralyze or propel you. Fear was my closest friend, pain my confidant, and sadness the condition of my soul. From as early as I could remember, this was the life I had known.

I saw the world through a lens dimmed with dark, murky, gray shadows, colored by rare and evasive glimpses of love, joy, and sunshine. Mostly, I felt helpless, hopeless, confused, and alone. What's the meaning of life? This was the question my small mind was asking yet could not fully formulate nor verbalize. Even if I could ask the question, with whom would I inquire? My connection with my mother was elusive, and my father was a farce. Silence was my ally.

## A Child's Worst Nightmare

I was about three or four years old when my mother phoned me while I was temporarily living in my grandparents' home. I eagerly climbed up on the high stool to reach the bright yellow rotary telephone and in an excited yet questioning shy voice said, "Hello?"

I recall my mother's uncomfortable, yet gentle voice on the other end say, "Hi, I miss you ... Do you miss me? Do you want me to come and see you?"

"Yes," I replied with excitement, overshadowed by a feeling of nervous disbelief.

Her response was, "I can't right now, but soon."

That conversation provided me no more comfort than I had prior to being absorbed in whatever I was doing before the call. Disappointed, I simply moved on as best as a child could.

Children have a resiliency about them, sort of a bounce-back program intrinsically coded within. No wonder we are told, *"unless you become like a child, you will never enter the Kingdom of Heaven"* (Matthew 18:3). I was around five years old when I moved in with my mother and my brother who is two years younger than me. I thought he was lucky to have our biological father's last name. I carried the last name of the man who had almost killed me, until I was finally released from it by my first marriage at the age of twenty-six.

My mother worked hard to keep a roof over our heads and food in our mouths. The rooves changed often, but the sadness within me remained the same. She was single, and as with many young, single women looking for love in all the wrong places, she spent a lot of time seeking excitement and the approval of men.

One unsuspecting day after I arrived home from elementary school, I was surprised to find all our clothes in oversized brown trash bags in the middle of the living room floor. My mom said with excitement, "We're moving!" I was confused. There was no warning and I had no idea where we were going. We moved in with two men. They were twins, and my mother was dating one of them. It was a hostile environment. There were drugs involved and domestic abuse. Thankfully, our stay was short-lived.

No matter where you go, there you are. My mother may have escaped that environment, but the pain she carried inside was ever-present and seemingly inescapable. My brother and I would witness her attempts to suppress it. A common scene was her coming home drunk late at night, or seeing her sprawled out across the couch, sleeping into the late afternoon. I wanted to look up to her. I wanted to feel safe. I wanted to feel the nurturing warmth of my mother's love. But I was just dreaming; my reality felt more like a nightmare.

## Invasions of Innocence

I was five years old when we lived in the top apartment of a duplex in Compton, California. My aunt and two older female cousins lived in the complex below ours. The older of the two was verbally and sometimes physically abusive, particularly while combing my thick and brittle hair. She used excessive force while laughing at my discomfort. We were often left in her care after school. It infuriated me when she made my brother and I watch *The Addams Family* or *Frankenstein* for hours and hours in that dark, eerily quiet apartment. There were plenty of nights when we'd stay over for whatever reason. This is when the sexual abuse began. I hated being made to touch my sacred parts—or hers. But, in my mind, I had to.

My mother had a girlfriend with whom she hung out regularly. Her friend also had two children, a girl and boy around the same ages as my brother and I. Our mothers would go out late at night, leaving the four of us to our own devices. We couldn't have been more than six to nine years of age when we discovered pornography on the television and decided to begin mimicking and exploring our sexuality together. This became a ritual for the four of us on the occasions when we were left alone together. We excitedly expected to play hide-and-go-get-it or spin-the-bottle.

By the time I was seven, masturbation had become ritual. Orgasms made me feel better. They gave me a place to escape the pain, sadness, and confusion of this world. It was one of the few things that felt really, really good. Orgasms ultimately gave me that "out of this world" experience I was looking for. I would always return to earth with insurmountable guilt, shame, and essentially more pain. The more I ran to my escape, the more I wanted to hide. I was conflicted. My innocence was gone.

One night, my little brother and I were being babysat at our cousins' downstairs apartment. They were having a party while my aunt was away. A few of their guy friends were invited over and I was being forced to drink alcohol. They were all laughing at me and taunting me while my mind was spinning with drunkenness. I couldn't have been more than ten years old. My poor younger brother was absolutely petrified! I can still see the look of terror in his eyes when he witnessed what would happen next.

Apparently, I'd gotten so drunk that one of their male friends who could have been no less than eighteen years old had somehow gotten me into the bedroom of the small apartment. I do not remember how I got there; all I remember is coming out of a blackout to find him lying on his back, sprawled across the bed with his pants hanging down and his penis in my mouth. I immediately sprang up and ran for the bathroom in terror and disgust where I would vomit everywhere! In hindsight, it was probably my brother's scream of horror that jolted me out of my drunken trance.

*"What sorrow awaits you who make your neighbors drunk! You force your cup on them so you can gloat over their shameful nakedness." ~Habakkuk 2:15 NLT*

As I attempted to clean myself up in the bathroom and recover emotionally from what had occurred, all I could see and hear was laughter from everyone present (With the exception of my brother, of course, who was crying, visibly shaken, and threatening to tell our mother the next day). This was no willing act of mine. Without hesitation, I told on myself the very next day. One part of me wanted to see my mother punish them, the other wanted her to console me. I do not know much of what happened next, but I do know the punishment did not fit the crime.

Not more than a year later, I recall being absolutely elated to speak to my father over the phone. On this particular day, he would be calling me from a drug rehabilitation center. I was eleven years old. I'd only seen or spoken to my father a handful of times prior to this day. I remembered him as always having been gentle, kind, and loving towards me.

Within minutes, our conversation took a sharp turn off the well-lit, straight and narrow path of innocent love, onto the path of deviant darkness. My father began speaking to me in a deep, soft, and raspy voice. He was asking me to touch myself and saying other sexual expletives. While nothing about touching myself while on the phone with my father was appealing to me, I confusingly pretended to play along until I heard what seemed to be his climax on the other end of the phone. Our phone call ended awkwardly and abruptly just moments after he returned to his senses.

## Defining Moments

It is astonishing how so few incidents can become the anchors of our self-identity. One of the books I read in the beginning of my transition from the flesh to the spirit was Dr. Phil's book, *Self*

*Matters*. In it, he points out that our personalities are comprised of roughly ten defining moments. Scientists are now bringing forth quantifiable evidence that we come into this life with a remanence of the unsolved mysteries of our ancestors written on our DNA. Religion would call this a generational curse.

If you want to change your life, it is imperative that you take time to reflect not only on the experiences you've had, but also their connection to the repeated patterns in your family of origin. It would take me more than a decade to figure out that this single phone call with my father, which couldn't have lasted more than five minutes, marks a deeply profound defining moment in my life. This brief, yet powerful exchange of energy had helped shape the way I saw myself and my value in the world. I adopted a sense of self deeply rooted in my flesh.

You may have responded to sexually-rooted defining moments by being promiscuous like I did. Or you could have gone the opposite way and steered clear of sex or romantic, emotional connection altogether. Perhaps you are confused about your sexuality and you keep tracing it back to a time when you were sexually violated. I am not saying that all gay, lesbian, or LGBTQ people have been molested or sexually abused. More on that later, but I do want to point out that whether you are heterosexual or any other sexual orientation, there is a sacred way to be in a sexual relationship that brings life and health. And there is also a way that breeds death and destruction.

*"Take no part in the unfruitful works of darkness, but instead expose them." ~Ephesians 5:11 ESV*

For me, the seeds of sexual deviancy, seduction, and lust had been planted. For almost half of my life, I watered the seeds and bore the fruit. It would take patience, pain, tears, grace, hope, faith, and love to dig up the weeds, sow new seeds, and reap a new harvest in my life. I wrote this book to tell you that not only is it possible for you to transcend the flesh, but you can do it *now*.

Your defining moments may not have come through the experience of inappropriate sexual conduct. They may have come by way of verbal, physical, or emotional abuse. You may not have received the love and support you would have expected from someone when you needed it most. You might be struggling to find a relationship with God because no one connected you with the idea of a Supreme Being in your youth. Or, on the contrary, your religion may have connected you with feelings of fear and self-disapproval because who you are at your core rubs up against their religious laws. Whatever your defining moments, I invite you to glance back and redefine the moments, so that the moments may no longer define you.

The first step in redefining your painful life experiences is to acknowledge that, as stated before, sin is simply a transgression against Universal Law. People generally transgress because they were taught to transgress and are ignorant of any other way. This is what it means to be born in sin. Let's take me for example. I experienced the impact of sexual misconduct at a very early age. This sexual energy was deposited into me through these acts, and very probably even before I was born. I repeated those acts out of ignorance, not knowing a better way.

I was a hurt person, hurting other people. Then I discovered God's grace and the love of a spiritual brother many call Jesus, who would bring me flowers when it rained and lift me up when I had fallen down. It was a transformative *defining moment* for me when I finally understood that no matter how erroneous the sins of my past, I was saved by grace—if only I spoke of my weakness and carried on in faith.

*"But he said to me, 'My grace is sufficient for you, for my power is made perfect in weakness.' Therefore, I will boast all the more gladly of my weaknesses, so that the power of Christ may rest upon me." ~2 Corinthians 12:9 ESV*

# Chapter 2: Your Sexy Is Sacred

*The blemishes on my face*
*Perfectly hidden by creamy cake*
*Cannot cover the disgrace*
*my preoccupation with the flesh has caused me*
*The vanity within me had revealed so very clearly*
*There's an enemy within who seeks to take my very breath*
*The lure of beauty and sensual play*
*Flaunting, my human on display*
*Resulted much to my dismay to be far less than what I wanted*
*Did I desire be consumed? An alluring piece of meat?*
*Reduced to breasts, a bubbly bottom,*
*Seductive eyes and mile high cheeks?*
*Pillaged, plundered, and impeached*
*From the throne of God by man?*
*Drunken, drowning in strong drink*
*Never once I stopped to think, of the demons,*
*they lurked and creeped all around me*
*Once without, now within, I was dying in my sin*
*Once I'd vowed never again!*
*Yet, it surrounds me*
*Oh the sorrow that next day*
*Crying, thunderous tears, I pray*
*The shame, the guilt, defeat*
*I lay there, silently*
*The enemy screaming in my head*
*"He'll never forgive you*
*You should be dead*
*God spoke more gently when SHe said*

*HEr grace is with me*
*Unconcealed before God naked*
*"Child of God, your sexy is sacred*
*I give new life; now will you take it?"*
*So, I did*
*~Sabrina Universal Lawton*

## Sex and Intimacy

From the time I was twelve, I sought men to make me feel whole, worthy, and valuable. I had a few "boy" friends, but I preferred long-term relationships with men who were well into their twenties. Boys weren't ready for the "real love" I was seeking. My innocence was taken at such a young age that I knew well by now how to *act* like a woman.

I learned to walk tall and use my external beauty and my natural gift of articulating a sweet, sultry string of words to grab the attention of men. I found many men to be intrigued by me, and while this did stroke my ego, it was always a temporary high. What I hadn't realized was that I really wanted someone to love me enough to see my pain and tell me I was okay.

I wanted intimacy, but I was confused about what it was. What do you imagine intimacy to be? Most people think of a romantic relationship, sensuality, and sex. Those things can be byproducts of intimacy, but they are not the seeds at the core.

Intimacy is rooted in a sacred connection between two people where each person sees into the very depths of the other's soul. Intimacy is experienced when two people can trust one another enough to say, "in-to-me—see." An intimate relationship is one in which you can hear each other's truths, empathize with each other's pain, embrace each other's vulnerabilities and imperfections, and love one another in the midst of it all.

Now wouldn't you want to have fantastic sex with a person like that? These are the necessary ingredients for a sacred soul-tie! Unfortunately, I wouldn't know this until after mounds of emotional pain had piled up miles high and all came crashing down in my thirties.

Prior to my awakening, my wires were all crossed. I had confused lust with love. Who was it that broke my virginity anyway? Perhaps you could say my virginity was broken at the tender age of five—or was it at seven? What I do know is that it was against my very will. It was a transgression against my soul, and an act of violence against my body.

It would take decades for me to reconcile my human experiences with my spiritual truths. Until that time, I walked through life in pain and ignorance, transgressing against man in the same way man had transgressed against me. The ultimate transgression was against my spirit.

*"For the desires of the flesh are against the Spirit, and the desires of the Spirit are against the flesh, for these are opposed to each other, to keep you from doing the things you want to do." ~Galatians 5:17 ESV*

## Looking for Love in all the Wrong Places

Although I experienced a tumultuous childhood, I always felt there was something very different, or for a better word, *unique* about me. I did not know the magnitude of my gifts and I used them to serve man and not God. I'd run from one sexually charged relationship to another, looking for love in all the wrong places and faces.

While the beginnings of my lustful endeavors tasted as sweet as honey, the bitterness of death would churn in my stomach without fail. No matter how hard I tried, I could not shake it. I persisted in running to the thing that was killing me inside.

*"There is a way that appears to be right, but in the end it leads to death."~Proverbs 14:12 NIV*

STD's like Chlamydia, Herpes, and HPV (Human Papilloma Virus) are more common than not. Rather than pass judgment, see them for what they are. These diseases are the collective fruit of our looking for love in all the wrong places. My sexual behaviors caused me to be deathly afraid of HIV/AIDS, which, thankfully, is no longer a death sentence. Many people are living long, happy, and healthy lives with proper care.

But I was so guilt-ridden that I feared if an STD wasn't going to take me out, I would get some other life-threatening disease as part of my well-deserved punishment. I was afraid of myself. I was afraid of God. Nevertheless, I continued my inappropriate behavior because I was mostly afraid of being sad and alone. I did not love myself, and I was on the constant quest for someone else to do it.

When I was fourteen years old, I met a beautiful, tall, dark-skinned boy named Elijah. He wore glasses and his appearance of "intellect" appealed to my senses. I recall several seductive encounters, but I remember the last one most. We went to his parents' place—and of course they were not home—and had quite passionate sex. I was proud of my amazing performance! In my mind, I'd conquered another male. He couldn't hurt me because now I was his drug. I knew he'd soon return for another fix.

Sex can be so engaging that you enter into a sort of tunnel vision and might not notice things you would otherwise be aware of. After Elijah and I had sex, I was shocked to see the unsightly rug burns on my knees, the consequence of our "doing it" on the bare carpets of his living room floor. He drove me home shortly thereafter. I was not expecting what I would say as I exited his car, nor do I think was he. I turned around, peered through the passenger side window, and eyed him with a smirk. I proceeded to throw a condom towards him and said, "Next time use a rubber," before walking away all nonchalant.

He called me later that day. I could hear the fear in his voice when he asked, "Why'd you do that, do I need to know something?"

My response was, "Uh nooooo, I just wanted to remind you to have safe sex, that's all." Honestly, at the time, I had no idea why I did or said that. Obviously, I had the condom, so why didn't I honor myself in advance by having him use it? This was a terribly selfish attempt to rid myself of emotional pain by passing it along to someone else.

This would be the theme of my life. Dating guys, ditching school, having sex, and getting into trouble with my mother for *"screwing up again"* (only the language she used was harsher). No matter how much attention I'd get, how many "relationships" I'd enter, or how much fun I'd have, I always felt empty in the end. I'd later come to find that this void was a God-shaped hole. The only way to fill it would be to stop looking for love in all the wrong places and start facing myself in the mirror. Easier said than done, as proven by the late, Michael Jackson.

## Why Lust Never Lasts

I so desperately wanted something different, but where would I begin? I was the blind leading the blind. I was the child teaching the child in the way that she should go. I sought love at home, yet did not find it. I felt loved by my grandmother as a child, but as I grew older, the constraints of her religion were too much for me.

Their mandates were things like don't celebrate most holidays, don't have sex before marriage, don't say hallelujah, don't watch this or that …They made the claim that no other religion is the "truth," and so on. There was far too much man-made law, judgment, and sacrifice in it for me. Besides, my eyes had seen and lips had tasted the seductive illusion of love by way of lust.

Surging through my DNA was a powerful elixir of sexual deviancy. Just as medical disease can run in families, so too can spiritual disease, which can present itself as lust, addiction, pessimism, suicidal tendencies, racism, and the list goes on and on. Thankfully, you are not at the mercy of your genetic code. You have the power to either activate or deactivate many of the programs written into your DNA.

One very necessary goal of your embarking on this journey with me is that you identify the seeds that were planted in your family tree. Dig up bad roots, cut off and throw into the branches the ideas, programs, thought patterns, and behaviors which do not serve you. Endure the fiery trials which help to usher us into change and clear the path for planting new seeds and bearing good fruit in your life. You have the opportunity of a lifetime to be the catalyst for a sharp shift in your family pathology. Take it for the sake of yourself and those who will follow you.

*"I am the vine; you are the branches. If you remain in me and I in you, you will bear much fruit; apart from me you can do nothing." ~John 15:5 ESV*

Because you are born of the Universe, you are calibrated to benefit most abundantly when you use your physical vessel to function in alignment with the *Universal Laws of Love*. The Law is simply this: *Love God and Love Yourself.* Only then can you truly love your neighbor. If you are like me, loving yourself seems to be the most difficult thing for you to do.

Women spend billions of dollars in the beauty and fashion industries, and men spend massive amounts of energy seeking wealth and sex to mask feelings of unworthiness and confusion about their purpose in life. Just look around you and see how our world is a reflection of who we truly believe we are.

*"You, my brothers and sisters, were called to be free. But do not use your freedom to indulge the flesh; rather, serve one another humbly in love." ~Galatians 5:13-14 NIV*

Globally, we suffer the consequences of our inability to *keep our sexy sacred*. Our largest societies are flooded with sex trafficking, child abuse, pornography, genital mutilation of girls and women, domestic violence, and other crimes of the flesh and, essentially, the spirit.

AIDS is an epidemic in many large countries where people do not have access, nor the means, to pay for proper medical care. You cannot drive down the streets, turn on your TV, or scroll down your social media feed without consuming sexual overtones and innuendo.

The more we feed it, the hungrier the spirit of lust becomes. Lust never lasts because while sex is a gift from God and an amazing, out-of-this-world experience, the *orgasm* will always be a poor substitute for the *Omega*.

## "Acts" of Pleasure

When one cannot access the love of God, which provides a pleasure that reaches far beyond the limitations of the human senses, sex can become an "artificial god." *"You cannot partake of the table of the Lord and the table of demons."* (1 Corinthians 10:21). As with all worship of false idols, overindulgence begins to energetically block your access to the Divine Essence of God through which *"you live and move and have your being."* (Acts 17:28).

The temporary high offered by sex alone can never fill the "God-shaped hole" which only a spiritually attuned life can fill. As with any drug, the immediate euphoria is followed by a painful, empty low, and as with most addicts, you soon find yourself seeking your next fix. The longer you remain an addict, the more of the drug you consume; yet, you never really experience the high you had in the beginning. Your appetite becomes insatiable.

Those addicted to sex and seduction tend to increase their promiscuous behaviors by practicing unsafe sex, having affairs, or escalating to orgies and other deviant sexual activities in attempts to stay high. I mention this not to guilt-trip anyone. You have free will; do as you please. Remember, however, that the Universe is self-correcting. Divorce, rape, sex-trafficking, and STD viruses are the manifestations of humanity's collective and unconscious attempts at seeking pleasure without understanding the *pleasure principles.*

Contrary to what the media, marketing, and advertising agencies tell you, sex is not love, and love is not sex—and both are still widely misunderstood. *"God sees not as man sees. Man looks on the outward appearance, but God looks on the heart."* (1 Samuel 16:7). The deception is real. The numbers don't lie. Adultery remains at the top of the list for why many marriages end in divorce. Hollywood has created a mass illusion that the rich guy gets the pretty girl, and the highlight of the super woman's super power is her outer beauty.

Think of your favorite television program. Do you see the drama, sex, vanity, greed, violence, pain, loss, and disappointments? Do these stories normally end in victory for those involved? While popular TV can be very entertaining, these shows are informing us of what *is* happening in our homes, businesses, churches, governments, and societies at large. The emotional, physical, and spiritual consequences in the real lives of the people, children, families, churches, and governments in these scenarios do not end with each episode.

Erectile dysfunction was once a condition that affected men in their forties and older. It is now affecting men in their early twenties. Pornography is a primary suspect. I've watched porn, so

36

I know the images very well. Let's take a not-so-graphic, typical sex scene. A man is having intercourse with a woman. He is banging her hard and fast as she's screaming at the top of her lungs and moaning in alleged ecstasy. Get the picture? Now let's reconcile this image to our collective reality.

When it comes to acts of pleasure, the fantasy is not nearly as pleasurable as the picture screens portray. In many a bedroom, there are sexless marriages, and many women are having sex with their husbands as an act of service. More marriages than you might imagine are sexless. The female clitoris is getting little to no attention and many women have gotten really good at faking orgasms. A recent Cosmopolitan survey revealed that of the 2,300 women polled, only 15 percent of them achieved orgasm via sexual intercourse alone, and 67 percent of these women also reported faking orgasms with their partners.

The vagina and penis are comprised of the same organs assembled in a different way. The woman benefits greatly from the change in design as the female clitoris has 8,000 nerve endings, roughly twice the amount of nerves in the male penis. Women generally require clitoral stimulation, as penile intercourse alone will not meet most women's anatomic criteria for orgasm. Did you know the word "clitoris" is the Greek word for "key?" Could it be that the clitoris is the key to more deeply understanding women's sexuality? Men would do women a great service by being good gentlemen and taking the initiative to unlock the door to the female orgasm.

I believe that God, in HEr infinite wisdom, designed it this way to ensure that virtues like patience, selflessness, trust, presence, and other high-vibrational frequencies of love be a prerequisite for good love-making. What is the difference between sex and love-making? I will share some pleasure principles you may want to consider when answering this question for yourself.

## Pleasure Principles

As you can probably imagine, I spent a good bit of my life seeking pleasure through romantic, sexually-driven relationships. I've also straddled the line a time or two with a one-night stand, a few affairs, excessive masturbation, and pornography. And with all that *pleasure,* I felt so much pain. Brother, if this is you, I understand. Sister, if this is you, I have been there too. After a series of unfortunate events that I will sprinkle throughout the following chapters, I decided to die to the flesh and be born again of the Spirit. Just as John the Baptist had prophesied, I have been baptized by the Holy Spirit and the fiery trials of my life.

*"I baptize you with water for repentance. But after me comes one who is more powerful than I, whose sandals I am not worthy to carry. He will baptize you with the Holy Spirit and fire."*
*~Matthew 3:11 NIV*

When I became new, what I experienced sexually surprised me. The ecstasy and pure bliss I felt as I joined in flesh and spirit with my second husband, Eric, who is the love of my life of now eleven years, did not come by way of my *performance.* Instead, I asked God to come to bed with us. I called upon the feminine energy of God to help me embrace and receive the love my husband was offering me. Sex is a bonding agent, weaving together the energies of two souls as one. This is one of the reasons why happily married couples begin to look alike.

As I thoroughly enjoyed the pleasure my husband was offering me, I was not screaming out of control to the point that I couldn't connect with my own bodily sensations. On the contrary, the ecstasy of our sexy, sacred experiences often brought me to silence. The airy, oceanic sound of each breath, interrupted by unplanned, high-pitched melodies that would flow effortlessly through my being was indeed a *celebration of love.* A key principle for having truly pleasurable sex resides in your awareness that when you engage in *"sex"* you are either engaging in a satanic or a *"sacred energy exchange."*

Men truly want to please. Many men still have that little boy inside who wants to hear, "great job," "you can do it," "I believe in you." Men are vulnerable children of God who have feminine energy, or estrogen, just as women have masculine energy, or testosterone. The problem is that our society has not given men the green light to feel, nor express, their emotions.

Men have collectively attempted to override this spiritual deficit by giving women "good sex" or making "good money" or being "the boss." The oxymoron is this: how can men give women good sex when they collectively do not understand our anatomy? Is the wealthy older man with the pretty young thing really fulfilled by her fake orgasms and "acts" of pleasure?

If you are unclear about whether or not you are in a sacred energy exchange with a person, you can gain clarity by asking yourself if the following key pleasure principles exist in your relationship:

## The Person:

- Lifts you up
- Energizes you
- Is there when you call
- Is someone you can trust
- Is *spiritually* connected with you
- Enjoys your company, with and without sex
- Knows who you *really are*, and loves you just the same

## Love is The Way

*"And so we know and rely on the love God has for us. God is love. Whoever lives in love lives in God, and God in them."*
*~1 John 4:16 NIV*

Now that we've cleared up some things about sex, what if I told you that sex, physical attraction, and money were highly overrated? What if you are guaranteed to create a life of abundance in every area of your life, including these, by simply doing one thing? Embrace the fact that *you* are the temple of God.

Stand in your god-power by loving yourself. Can you love yourself through the anger, the pain, the guilt, the addiction, the shame? Will you love yourself in the disappointment, the despair, the grief, the loss, the failure? Or will you run from person to person, looking for someone else to do it for you?

In my work as a Spiritual Advisor, I am honored to connect with women who were single and brokenhearted, fathers going through divorce, and influential people who had achieved success in the material world, but their private lives were in pieces. By the time our work is done, the women are happily married, the men enjoy loving relationships with their children, and the influential people have a much more positive impact on those they lead because they themselves have evolved. You might be wondering what magic formula I use. There is no magic. Tricks are for kids. The *miracle* is the experience of how quickly God will turn your life around when you embody the *Universal Laws of Love*.

*"But seek first the kingdom of God and his righteousness, and all these things will be added to you." ~Matthew 6:33 ESV*

# Chapter 3: Sex—The Forbidden Fruit

*"The greatest damage is that [over-indulgence] depletes the source of man's driving force, and wastes, without compensation, man's creative energy." ~Napoleon Hill: Outwitting the Devil*

Why is it that in the twenty-first century, with all our technological advances, space travels, understanding of complex algorithms, and spiritual enlightenment movements, sex is still such a huge thorn in our side? The answer may completely rock your world! The irony is that the answer has always been here in plain sight, right before our eyes. ***Sexual immorality was the forbidden fruit in the Garden of Eden.*** It was the fruit from the tree of the knowledge of good and evil which God forbid HEr firstborn children to partake of. Let's take another look at the *original* sin story through unfiltered lenses.

Adam and Eve were in the Garden of Eden and all was heavenly bliss. They were made in the image and likeness of God. They were given dominion over the fish in the sea, the birds in the sky, the livestock, and all creatures that moved along the ground. Like gods, they had free will. They were also given a commandment ... "thou shalt not eat from the tree of the knowledge of good and evil." (Genesis 2:17).

Take a moment to review a few of the many references to "trees and fruit" in the Bible:

- "Beware of false prophets, who come to you in sheep's clothing but inwardly are ravenous wolves. You will recognize them **by their fruits.** (Matthew 7:15, emphasis added).

- "**Filled with the fruit** of righteousness that comes through Jesus Christ, to the glory and praise of God." (Philippians 1:11, emphasis added).

- "Abide in me, and I in you. **As the branch cannot bear fruit by itself,** unless it abides in the vine, neither can you, unless you abide in me. **I am the vine; you are the branches.** Whoever abides in me and I in him, he it is that **bears much fruit**, for apart from me you can do nothing." (John 15:4-7, emphasis added).

- "Even now the axe is laid to the root of the trees. **Every tree therefore that does not bear good fruit** is cut down and thrown into the fire." (Luke 3:9, emphasis added).

- "The [blind] man looked around. 'Yes,' he said, 'I see people, but I can't see them very clearly. **They look like trees** walking around.'" (Mark 8:24, emphasis added).

You've likely picked up on the fact that the "fruit" and "trees" mentioned in the above scriptures are actually referencing the spiritual condition of humankind. As for the last bullet point, do you really believe that Jesus made a mistake the first time he attempted to heal the blind man who initially saw people as walking trees? I think not.

Jesus frequently taught with analogies and parables. He likely wanted us to know that humans function much like trees. Our roots are grown from the seeds sown by our thoughts and beliefs; our branches reflect our actions, the things we do as a result of our beliefs. The quality of our lives, good or bad, is a reflection of the fruit we ourselves have produced.

Now that you have a new foundation upon which to understand the original sin, let's get back to the command that God gave Adam and Eve: "you shall not eat of the fruit of the tree of the knowledge of good and evil." At this particular point in the juncture of creation, God had made all things good. There was but one entity cast down to earth who had both the knowledge of good and evil … Lucifer.

## Strange Fruit

Lucifer, who has many names—the Devil, Satan, and the Accuser to name a few—was right there in the beginning of all creation. He was adorned with every precious stone of onyx, jasper, emerald, and more. He was appointed guardian cherub until wickedness was found within him.

*"Your heart was proud because of your beauty; you corrupted your wisdom for the sake of your splendor. I cast you to the ground; I exposed you before kings, to feast their eyes on you."*
*~Ezekiel 28:17 ESV*

With regard to the "fruit," the serpent said to the woman, "You will not surely die. For God knows that when you eat of it your eyes will be opened, and you will be like God, knowing good and evil." When the woman saw that the tree was good for food, and that it was a delight to the eyes, and that the tree was to be desired to make one wise, she took of its fruit and ate, and she also gave some to her husband **who was with her,** and he ate.

*"At that moment their eyes were opened, and they suddenly felt shame at their nakedness. So they sewed fig leaves together to cover themselves." ~Genesis 3:7 NLT*

Is it possible that Eve partook of the fruit of Satan's *being?* Is it probable that a human had an encounter, sexual in nature, with a demon? This would explain those cartoony caricatures of a demonic male having sex with a human woman frequently advertised on many pornographic websites. Let's review the immediate consequences of their sin:

- "Then the eyes of both were opened, and they knew that they were naked. And they sewed fig leaves together and made themselves loincloths." (Genesis 3:7, emphasis added).

- **The Lord God said to the serpent:** "I will put enmity between you and the woman, and between your offspring and her offspring; he shall bruise your head, and you shall bruise his heel." (Genesis 3:15, emphasis added).

- **To the woman he said:** "I will surely multiply your pain in childbearing; in pain you shall bring forth children. Your desire shall be contrary to your husband, but he shall rule over you." (Genesis 3:16, emphasis added). 2

- **And to Adam he said:** "Because you have listened to the voice of your wife and have eaten of the tree of which I commanded you, 'You shall not eat of it,' cursed is the ground because of you; in pain you shall eat of it all the days of your life; thorns and thistles it shall bring forth for you; and you shall eat the plants of the field. By the sweat of your face you shall eat bread, till you return to the ground, for out of it you were taken; for you are dust, and to dust you shall return." (Genesis 17:19, emphasis added).

## Let's Recap:

- Adam and Eve immediately felt *shame* at their nakedness
- There would be enmity between Satan's offspring and Eve's
- Childbirth would be painful
- Eve's desire shall be contrary to her husband, but he shall rule over her
- The man would work hard all the days of his life, yet have no real peace of mind

Notice that these consequences are all related to areas of intimacy, relationship, and sexuality—and the battle of the sexes continues. Take note, Adam did not rule over Eve when she was created, just as the animals who were created before Adam had no dominion over him. This was merely a consequence of sin, for which Jesus paid the price.

Just because Eve was the last in all creation doesn't make her less than Adam. If you ask me, I'd say the more God created, the more magnificent the creation became, right up to the climax, the exclamation, the crescendo of all creation: *Woman*. Clearly, Satan took note of her power and majesty—to the point that he wanted to join with her.

Now if this isn't proof enough that humans and fallen angels engaged in sexual intermingling at the beginning of time, the following scripture will:

*"And the angels who did not stay within their own position of authority, but left their proper dwelling, he has kept in eternal chains under gloomy darkness until the judgment of the great day—just as Sodom and Gomorrah and the surrounding cities, which likewise indulged in sexual immorality and pursued unnatural desire, serve as an example by undergoing a punishment of eternal fire." ~Jude 1:6-7 ESV*

## The Nature of Evil

*"Whoever makes a practice of sinning is of the devil, for the devil has been sinning from the beginning. The reason the Son of God appeared was to destroy the works of the devil."*
*\~1 John 3:8 ESV*

There is a powerful punch packed into this Bible verse! It informs us that when we make a *practice* of sinning or doing things that cause harm, we are of the devil. To practice a thing is to repeat what you learned in your *past.* If in your past, you learned to connect with feelings of guilt, shame, judgement, sexual immorality, low self-esteem, and other negative emotions, you will be inclined to repeat behaviors that recreate the feelings you have unconsciously associated with yourself. For this reason, evolving beyond your past is a necessity. Within this truth resides the following *divinity code*: To live backwards is to experience evil *(live-evil).* We have all lived backwards; therefore, we have all known the devil *(lived-devil).*

Satan can only tempt you with the same things you have fallen for over, and over, and over again in your past. He knows you're running a program and has just the right treats to trick you. There is but one problem. Everything evil does is backwards, and your inviting it in will eventually have no choice but to backfire on you. The time is now for us to collectively shift our focus from

46

merely living to loving. The Presence of Love is always here, now. Not in the past where woulda', shoulda', and coulda' live.

When the spirit of Satan was cast down, he was not alone; he brought with him a legion. We know that just as surely as the Holy Spirit resides within each one of us, demons can also take up residence. In the Bible, there are several accounts of demons being cast out. In one account, there was a man with an unclean spirit within him. To the demon Jesus commanded, "Come out of the man, you unclean spirit!" And Jesus asked him, "What is your name?" He replied, "My name is Legion, for we are many." (Mark 5:8-9). The demons pleaded with Jesus to allow them to enter into the nearby pigs. Even the pigs couldn't handle the torment. They ran into a nearby lake and drowned.

What religion refers to as spirit, science may refer to as energy when it comes to things of a biological nature like you and me. You need not get caught up in semantics. Whether you refer to it as spirit or energy is no matter; neither energy nor spirit ever dies. Just as you and God are one, so too are energy and spirit inseparable. Who are you swapping your energy with? What energies or spirits are you allowing to be attached to you?

Science has proven that the DNA of every single person you have ever had sex with remains within you. No wonder having sex with a crazy person will threaten to drive you crazy! I am not here to tell you what you should or should not do. I am here to ask that you use your free will wisely because everything is energy and *spirits are transferable.*

If you know you are spirit, and you know that you do not fight against flesh and blood but other spirits, then you know you are always exchanging energy with either angels of Light or demons of Darkness. Serve two masters if you choose—just know the natural consequences of doing so.

*"No one can serve two masters: Either he will hate the one and love the other, or he will be devoted to the one and despise the other ..."* ~Matthew 6:24 NIV

For years, I served two masters. I was what the scriptures referred to as a double-minded person, unstable in all my ways. I searched high and low, sampling the seeds of men, looking for the good fruit that I thought would help me heal my pain. All the while I loved God and God loved me. Regardless of our misdeeds, God knows our hearts.

## Sleepless in Seattle

I was fifteen years old when I fled from Los Angeles, California to Seattle, Washington, where my mother had recently gotten married and relocated. I was running from a physically abusive relationship. After a few months of getting familiar with my new town, I met my son's father, Anthony, who was a twenty-eight-year-old man. We were at a local mall near the food court. I remember us walking straight past one another, and both of us glanced back at the same time and sort of shrugged, in a gesture that felt like: *well okay, we got nothin' better to do ...* Though he was attractive, he might not have been my first pick. He had a finger-wave and a shag for a hairstyle (don't ask), and I was going for the Halle Berry look. Truthfully, my haircut was more like a "hardly barely." Nevertheless, I was a lonely girl, still seeking shelter in the arms of a man.

I had practically moved in with Anthony by the time I was seventeen and became pregnant with our son Martin at eighteen years old. Anthony was a nice guy, but he had an obsessive personality. He would not have been my choice life partner, but, well, I thought he was really loyal to me ... I knew he'd be a good dad ... I was not exactly correct in my assumptions.

I discovered a lot more about Anthony while I was pregnant. This man who didn't seem to have a past, decided to inform me that I met him shortly after he was released from serving a six-year prison sentence for charges of assault and kidnaping in the second degree. He went on to say that when the crime was committed, he was suffering from an (undiagnosed at the time) bi-polar episode.

Entering the relationship, I knew he had one daughter who was about ten years old. What I did not know was that while he was in prison, another woman had come forth, alleging that he was the father of her roughly five-year-old daughter. Paternity was proven. Here I was, eighteen years old, pregnant by a man twelve years my senior who'd been to prison and had two other children of his own. It would have been great to have had a few more details before I chose him as my next desperate endeavor, but there is something called cause and effect. I'd later come to terms with the fact that I was not a victim. I was the creator of the cause, and the effects were my own to deal with.

One of the consequences of my tolerating Anthony's passive-aggressive, controlling behavior was the loss of a very sacred opportunity to bond more tightly as a mother with our son. Anthony spent most of my pregnancy giving me many compelling reasons why I should not breastfeed our son, Martin. He went on to tell me how technology had done its job, and that there were tons of perfectly manufactured formulas of milk out there to give our son the nutrients he needed. In my youth and naiveté, I believed him.

It took me a long time to figure out that Anthony was not concerned about the optimal health of our son; otherwise, he would have chosen the perfectly *formulated by God* milk that had been produced by my breasts. He was far more concerned about the possibility that a man might see my breasts in public.

*"Even jackals offer their breasts to nurse their young, but my people have become heartless like ostriches in the desert."*
*~Lamentations 4:3 NIV*

Other times he went on about why I shouldn't wear high heels, or go to the gym, or wear tight pants without tying a sweater around my waist to cover my butt. That should give you enough background information to know why I felt like a slave with tight chains around my hands and feet—and a chastity belt for good measure.

My loving master would say things like, *you know you don't want to be the way you were in the past. This is about a higher purpose. What do you think God would want you to do with your body? I love you and you love me ... Why would you want anyone to see... ?* Between the ages of eighteen and twenty-six, I dressed like a Quaker, which I guess would have been fine if I actually was one. I had no network of friends and we had no social life. Everyone around us could see his control tactics. Everyone but me.

While all the above was certainly true, I confess that I was no angel. I cheated on him a few times throughout our relationship. I even had a fling with a man who worked in the office where Anthony's father had given me my first real job. The pent-up frustrations of being with one man for years, with whom I had no real natural affection, became quite the thorn in my side. The affairs were my way of breaking free from the cage I felt I was locked in.

Anthony and I had a few break-ups and make-ups, but I found it ironic that he was never in a hurry to leave me. The beauty in it all is that God allowed Anthony to be my temporary guardian. He served his role at the time of protecting me from myself. I am grateful to him for that. Can you imagine how much more self-inflicted pain I could have caused if during those twelve years, I had been free to fly? As the late great poet Maya Angelou said, "I know why the caged bird sings."

What I loved about Anthony was that he was very concerned about issues affecting our community. He also enjoyed having conversations about God. We would talk for hours while smoking weed, or playing games on his PlayStation. We became active in the community, attending rallies and delivering speeches at local black community events. The year was 1999 when we joined with NAACP's Seattle local chapter MLK committee. We were on schedule to recite a poem entitled "United We Stand. Divided We Die."

I do not recall the entire poem, but I vividly remember how well it was received. As the day progressed, the crowd would come together to march from the inner city to downtown Seattle. After a few miles' walk, we stopped outside of Republican talk show radio station 570 KVI. As you'd expect from a protestors' type of rally, there was an undercurrent of frustration and agitation in the air. The MLK committee leaders were eagerly anticipating an on-air interview to discuss race relations.

Anthony and I were the new kids on the block. Everyone was stunned when the radio station staff specifically requested that Anthony and I be their guests for the live interview! While we were not in the least bit prepared, a sort of internal *knowing* came over me. My emotional posture was calm and at peace. Strangely, I felt right at home during the interview. It was as if something greater than me, yet within me, had automatically become activated.

Inside the studio, right on the wall behind the talk radio host, was what appeared to be a painting of four diversely different children. The host asked the question, "when you look at this picture, what do you see?" To the naked eye, one might have seen a perfectly painted portrayal of unity. What I saw was a group of what American society would call minorities. That was my prompt and certain response: "I see all minorities."

The talk show host gave me a puzzled look and asked me to elaborate. I continued to describe what I saw. There was a white

51

girl, an Asian girl, a Hispanic boy, and an African-American girl, but where was the white male child?

A momentary and uncomfortable silence fell upon the airwaves. A few more questions followed, and I was like Neo in the Matrix, ready to not run, nor duck, nor take up my defenses, but rather simply to stop the bullets, with my words as my wand, wearing the full armor of God. To my surprise, Anthony spoke very little throughout the entire interview. I felt strongly that it was I who took the lead, but I didn't mention it back then.

Decades later, I jokingly mentioned this to him during friendly conversation. Anthony confessed that his voice was taken that night and that he could not speak. Chills ran through my entire body at the sound of his truth. We never knew why, but the talk show host left his job at the radio station shortly after our interview.

Anthony and I hid our problems well from Martin, who was a beautiful, happy, loving, and very well-behaved child. For years, I'd concede to the idea that this was my life. The lie I was living was starting to feel like the truth. I really wanted to do things right. About eight years into our relationship, I thought it was time to stop postponing our marriage until we had enough money, or whatever other viable excuses we made.

I was in my mid-twenties when we finally wed. We divorced after just two years of matrimony. I cried on my wedding day. My tears were not tears of joy. Deep inside, I felt I'd just closed the door to any opportunity I would ever have to be in love. In a very real sense, I was mourning my life—the life I thought I'd never know.

As you can imagine, those two years were a struggle, and tensions were rising. The little girl inside me began to throw a temper tantrum! He was twelve years my senior. I did not want a father figure; I wanted a hot and steamy romance with someone I was really attracted to. I felt trapped with no way out.

That is, until I met the neighbor.

## A Neighborly Affair

As a wedding gift, Anthony's father gifted us with a down payment on a new home in a nice, lower-middle-class, family-oriented community. It was a beautiful, two-story, three-bedroom house at the end of a cul-de-sac. Anthony and I tried to build a family, but the foundation simply wasn't there. Within a few weeks of moving into our new home, the neighbor caught my eye.

There he was. This not-so-tall, handsome, deeply dark *"Melano"* young man just a few houses down. I use the term *Melano* to describe the dark pigmentation of melanin-dominant people. I prefer this truer, more glamorous term over the use of the term that has been *defamed* by man: *b-lack*. More on that later. Judging by his appearance, we were about the same age. He owned his home, kept his grass neatly manicured, and his haircut was just as sharp as the edges of his lawn, the top of his head adorned with shiny black curls.

The sleeping giant of lust that lived within me was quickly awakened, and it was hungry. I knew Micah had taken note of me as well. Within a couple months, we were having small talk at the community mailboxes. Our flirting escalated, and I'd muster up the guts to wear my tight-fitting jeans without the sweater to cover my butt (as my husband had always insisted). I also became fond of roller-blading around our small neighborhood, specifically during the times I expected him to return home from work.

During one of our brief mailbox chats, I asked him to meet me at a nearby bus station where I would leave my car to commute via mass transit to work each day. He did. A few days later, we met behind a local movie theater and had sex in his car. Next, in the guest bedroom of his house, then his living room, then his bedroom, and again and again. My mind was a dirty cocktail of seduction, lust, love, guilt, shame, and pain.

There was an addictive force continually fusing Micah and I together. We were knitted in an energetically entangled web of lust, lies, and secrecy. Our relationship was one created in the darkness, and I desperately wanted the light! I considered myself a Christian at the time. I knew my behavior was wrong. I was drowning in a deep sea of unworthiness and depression, which led to binge drinking, partying, and smoking cigarettes. It felt like self-annihilation, but I did it anyway. As much as I hated it, it was what I wanted. I had never felt so alive and so dead all at once. I was losing my mind.

In a desperate attempt to stop the affair, I told my husband what I had done. The neighbor was beyond livid at the fact that I would tell our juicy secret. Micah resolved to never-ever-ever have sex with me again—ever! But every time I'd knock, unsolicited and uninvited, it was like a trance would overtake him. He would always partake of the fruit I had to offer.

After about two years of our on-and-off affair, I was having a mental breakdown. My son was just eight when our affair began. His dad and I had done a fairly good job of hiding our relationship woes. We rarely raised our voices, and although we had our difficulties, we showered our son with love the best we knew how. But the curtains would soon begin to fall on this Bill Cosby Show of an illusion.

My affair affected my mental health with so much emotional toxicity that I could not function in my career, as a woman, a wife, nor as a mother. I'll never forget the day when my son was riding his bike in our cul-de-sac. He fell off his bike, sliding face-first into the concrete right in front of Micah's house. The unsightly bruise rushing down one side of his face was a stark reminder of how far I was from where I needed to be in my walk with God. Little did I know at the time—this affair would mark the beginning of the darkness, pain, trauma, and shame which would allow demons to take up residence in my unsuspecting son's life.

As much as I wanted to go back to life as it was before the affair, I knew that I could not remain with my husband. There was no regaining the status quo. The truth is that my affairs were my very immature way of trying to force my husband to leave me. It took a lot for him to say enough is enough, but he finally did, and he filed for divorced.

While I clearly wanted the divorce, I was now cast into what felt like the deepest, darkest abyss I'd ever known! From the time I was a teen, I had not been without a man to take care of me. I really had no idea who Sabrina was. During our divorce proceedings, I fought for custody, and, as you could imagine, I lost the battle. Admittedly, the cards were pretty stacked against me. It didn't help that Anthony used his father's resources to secure a lawyer. I had no one to come to my defense. Witnessing the pain Martin would endure as a result of his entire life being flipped upside-down was a living hell! It would take years of heartache and pain before I was able to mend my relationship with my son and hold his hand as he healed from the aftermath.

# Chapter 4: Love and Loss

I lost a lot in this game I chose to play. The most precious of my losses was my ability to be a strong, loving presence in Martin's life between when he was ten and sixteen years old. His father was granted primary custody and my visitation was reduced to weekends, which his dad used to monopolize his time with basketball games and dreams of going to the NBA.

The less time my son spent with me, the more I witnessed helplessly, him becoming everything I would never raised him to be. It caused me great agony to watch helplessly as my son became submerged in a wretched program running in many inner-city school gymnasiums across America. Hundreds of thousands of young Melano boys, fighting for their spot on one of the roughly thirty basketball teams across America. What are the odds of that?

To those who are currently in the grips of this program, *awaken*. The evil spirits flowing through the airways of our world have been turning your superpowers into a mockery, reducing you to mere entertainers of men. You are not entertainers of men. You are inspirers of God's greatness in all of humanity!

Parents, encourage your children to learn quantum physics and biology or any other discipline of the sciences. This will help them understand the fundamental building blocks of life. Understanding the science, or energy, of God will open their minds to see clearly the natural gifts they have to create a life and a world filled with exceedingly more peace, love, and prosperity than they can ask, think, or imagine.

Unless your child is being groomed to become like the far-too-few sports greats, who engage the system strong in spirit, sound in mind, and unshakeable in purpose, you are pouring their God-given gifts into banks that possess only the currency of greed and spiritual deficiency. Like far too many athletes who buy into this deception, in the end, they find themselves bankrupt.

I would spend four years in basketball gyms, painstakingly loving my son from the sidelines. This was a turbulent time in our relationship, and it hurt me terribly to know that I had played a role in helping my son's life become what it was. When Martin was fourteen, I received a phone call from a local elementary school informing me that my son and his dad were at open gym the night before. The person on the other line continued to disclose that they were in possession of video footage showing Anthony roughing up Martin in ways that reached beyond parental discipline.

I hurried to obtain the footage I would need to get my son back! I submitted the video to the courts and did whatever I had to do to get our parenting plan case reopened. Back and forth, I went to the courthouse, exhausted and frustrated with his father. With all the tension, anger, and hostility Martin's dad and I exchanged over what was best for our son, it was our son who would hang in the balance, desperately trying to balance his own scales.

By now, I'd just begun to scratch the surface of my spiritual healing work. I believed that God was offering me another opportunity to raise my son. For me, this was a silver lining. In a miracle of God, I was able to secure an attorney who took on my case without a retainer. Our parenting plan was subsequently revised, and I was awarded primary custody of our son. I was ecstatic! I felt as though a huge weight had been lifted from my shoulders! I thought Martin would just pack his bags, move out of his dad's, and allow me to help him get right back on track! I thought the battle was over, but the battle had just begun. My victory was short-lived.

A lot happened for me in those four years as a sideline mom. I remarried, had another child, and purchased a new home. You'll learn a lot more about my parallel life in just the turn of a page. Meanwhile, Martin had grown accustomed to a lifestyle and environment very different from my own. His father, Anthony never re-married and had also moved back into to his parents' home, in which Anthony was both born, and sadly, also recently died. May he rest in love.

Back then, I lived forty-five minutes south in a suburban, and largely Caucasian, community. My new husband, Eric, and I were met with much resistance caused by the glaring differences in the inner workings of each household. We spent massive amounts of energy trying to get Martin to see the light. We weren't just fighting for better grades, or for him to clean his room more often. We were fighting for his soul. It would be two grueling years before Martin decided to give our way a try. After a series of tough battles with the demons who tried to take up residence, we had finally begun to see the signs that we had won the war between the flesh and the spirit!

If I had to do it all again, I would walk through every fiery trial. I would fight through every tear, every agony, every hope deferred, and every valley and shadow of death to save our son from the maladaptive virus that had been programmed into his mind and become activated in his heart and soul. Their entrance, through trauma and pain. Their exit, through perseverance, hope, faith, and love. While my new husband and I did move mountains to save his soul. We are also aware that Martin's true salvation could only come by way of his own *personal relationship* with God.

*"For everyone who calls on the name of the Lord will be saved."~Romans 10:13 ESV*

## The Love of My Life

As promised, let's talk about my parallel life while I was in my season as a "sideline mom". It was New Year's Day and I hadn't gone out on New Year's Eve because I had visitation with my son and wanted to be fully present. The next day, I decided to ring in the New Year with some partying! When I arrived at the lounge, it was almost vacant. It dawned on me that everyone was probably hungover from the festivities the night before. There I stood, thinking to myself, "What have I done with my life? Maybe I should have stayed with my ex-husband? At least it was safe, and our son certainly seemed better off!"

The sharp pang of emptiness and misery was short-lived when moments later, a beautiful man with smiling eyes walked in. I instantly thought to myself, "Now I'd talk to him …Wait, is he walking straight towards me?" Sure enough, he did exactly that! He walked right up to me as if I were his only intention, and said, "Hi, may I buy you a drink?"

I smiled in a very interested way and said, "Sure … I think I know you."

He said, "You couldn't possibly know me, I've only lived in Seattle for two weeks."

Moments later, I said, "Eric."

He smiled confusingly and then looked in shock as he said, "Sabrina!"

"Yes," I replied with a huge smile.

I hadn't noticed when he was at a distance, but the closer he got, the more familiar he became. Eric and I double-dated during high school in Los Angeles, roughly fourteen years prior. That seemed like a lifetime ago! I hadn't thought about Eric more than a handful of times over the years. Why would I? I was into his friend back then, and he was hanging with my friend. As short-lived as our connection was back then, I knew I'd seen his face before.

## God's Plan

We went out on a few dates and hit it off quite well after I got over the fact that we had previously dated each other's friends. It was our third or fourth date when he leaned in and said, "Can I let you in on a little secret?" He told me about how he had driven almost two hours from the city of Olympia to Seattle the night we were reunited. He went on to say how disappointed he was about having taken such a long drive to have a good time and meet new friends, only to find a half-empty lounge and not a single soul with whom he wanted to engage in conversation.

He proceeded to tell me about how after a drink at the bar, he retreated to his car, and planned to make the long, lonely drive home. As fate would have it, his best friend called him while he was sitting in his car, key in the ignition. They were talking on the phone when Eric looked up and saw me standing at the crosswalk, right in front of his car. He sat there watching as I crossed the street and said to himself, "If she goes into that lounge, I'm going back in."

After fighting ideas of rejection, he finally resolved that he had nothing to lose. He had made up his mind. He was going to go back inside and walk right up to me, no games, no lurking, just clear intention. He never thought in a million years that he'd walk up only to hear me say, "I think I know you."

There is no such thing as coincidence. How can coincidence be a possibility when God knows the very number of hairs on your head and number of your days? I know with certainty that God planted the seeds of familiarity between Eric and I over a decade prior to help springboard us into the next chapters of our lives.

A deep, hot, two-to-three-times-a-day, sexy romance ensued. Eric and I were totally into each other! We started playing house rather quickly. Whenever I stayed the night, I could tell he really appreciated it when I made him turkey bacon, English muffins, and freshly-squeezed juice the next morning. Looking back, it all made sense. He had just ended a year-and-a-half deployment in Iraq, and I was just ending a deeply unfulfilling twelve-year relationship. It was the perfect storm and there was lots of thunder and lightning!

There was much more to us than sex. We truly enjoyed each other's company. One of the most memorable of our first dates was shortly after I had gotten fired from a corporate banking job where I had been a tax manager. On the surface, it appeared that I gotten fired because my employee had made a mistake that cost the company and I should have caught it. I knew deep down inside that the real reason I got fired was because my life had been spiraling out of control for quite some time and it was all finally catching up with me.

I wanted to hide under a rock and never come out. I was beyond embarrassed to share the news with my newfound love interest. When I finally mustered up the strength to tell him, I absolutely melted inside at his response, "Don't worry, just see it as an extended vacation." He went on to say, "Let's go flying." Eric had his pilot's license! A few days later, we set out for the skies! I enjoyed the amazing sights from the small plane after I had gotten over a twinge of nervous energy.

There's nothing like flying through a puff of white clouds! The sights were absolutely spectacular; however, the view I enjoyed the most on that day was of Eric. I studied him intently as he piloted the plane. I watched his lips as he spoke with Air Traffic Control through the mouthpiece attached to his headset. I watched his gorgeous eyes as he gazed out among the skies. I remember his call sign was Four Zero Tango Pappa. Oh yeah, pappa. I was ready to tango all right!

A couple months later, Eric's prediction about my employment status was confirmed. I got a new job working for one of the largest human capital companies in the United States. My new job also came with a twenty-thousand-dollar annual increase! Was I dreaming? Right in the midst of my storms, the presence of God seemed to be supporting my journey. Suddenly I had found a good man who could fly a plane, had a good job, was disciplined by the Army, slow to speak, a good listener, had no kids, and had never been married! Cha-Ching—Jackpot!

Ours is a beautiful love story. Today, we share the kind of love that many people dream of. As with most good love stories, there would be lots of pain, drama, and many rivers to cross before we reached our promised land. When Eric and I met, neither of us were aware that he would spend the next few years of our life toting my oversized bags of emotional distress, which well exceeded the standard limitations, while also handling his lightweight, carry-on luggage.

My life was in a state of rapid disassembly at the time. Not only had I lost primary custody of my son, I was losing my home and moving in with my mom. I was in the thick of divorce, and I partied and drank more than I should have. I was also in deep depression due to my carrying around years of trauma, guilt, shame, regret, and pain. I was figuratively lost in the sauce! Eric was my knight in shining armor who would give me life support.

About four months into our courtship, Eric informed me that he would be moving again in the very near future. Two years prior, he had applied with the FBI for a Federal Law Enforcement Officer position. He had received word the agency had begun interviewing his friends as part of their background check process. I felt my heart sink into the pit of my stomach when I heard the news. I quickly swallowed the swelling emotions of sadness, fear, and loss within me. My response was brief and resolute, "It was great knowing you. I do not do long-distance relationships without commitment. That'd be a waste of my time and yours."

Over the next two months, Eric prepared to relocate. I helped him rent out his home, and we continued our relationship with a focus on friendship. The day had finally arrived. Eric had relocated. As a job requirement, he would report to their training facilities in Brunswick, Georgia. After about a month had passed, my employer sent me to Alpharetta, Georgia for business travel. Eric did not hesitate to ask if he could pay me a visit. It would be about a five-hour drive from Brunswick—but a heck of a lot closer than Seattle!

During his visit, Eric asked for my hand in marriage! I will always remember how he proposed in the most beautiful way. There were three envelopes, each of them having drawings and clues as in a game of charades. The last card and clue, "Bugs Bunny needs one but you deserve one."

I yelled out a hurried and excited response, "A CARROT?"

Eric literally pulled out a carrot, like what you'd see in a Bugs Bunny cartoon, green leafy stem and all! My closed-eye, belly'rolling'over' laughter was interrupted when I found him on his knee with a diamond ring. Two carrots for good measure!

I said, "Yes!" It was a strange, scary, exciting, and what-did-I-just-do kind of moment. I was mostly happy; however, admittedly, I had thoughts like, "The ink isn't even dry on your divorce, Sabrina. Do you really love Eric like you think you do?" Even with all that noise, my most prevalent thought was about how spending the rest of my life with him just seemed right.

We thoroughly enjoyed our time together as a newly engaged couple. Our feel-good receptors were full speed ahead! We were in love. I returned to Seattle a few days later, only sadly, there was no Eric. Who would help me through my loneliness and depression? Who would give me something to smile about? I was absolutely miserable on my own, and my reality bit hard.

My mom was showing me through her own behavior everything that I did not want to be, yet, was becoming. It cuts to the core when a little girl spends her life longing for her mother to teach her how to be a woman but she can't because she's too busy trying to cater to the little girl inside her too. I hope my mother knows how much I understand. Many children, including my own, are impacted by our unhealed wounds as parents.

A few months after our engagement, Eric and I met up in Florida, where we planned an absolutely beautiful beach wedding for just the two of us. God, the wedding planners, and our ordained minister were the only witnesses of our marriage. It was the month of July. Little did we know this was the rainy season in Florida. It was less like rain and more like buckets of water being dumped out from the Heavens! The morning of July 7th had dawned; and our wedding day had arrived! It was still raining cats and dogs as we drove along the lone, seemingly never-ending road, in search of our beachfront wedding location.

I sat there silently, and on the brink of tears, as we drove along in our all-white beach wedding attire for what felt like an eternity. We finally arrived at our destination, graced by an ocean of turquoise waters. The sand was so hot that I could not walk across it without wearing my sandals. I looked up to find a huge hole in the sky with beautiful bright sunrays and electrifying heat peering through.

It was as if God was saying, "I am with you. I approve." We had a beautiful, *dry,* and what felt to be a very *sacred,* low-budget beach wedding. The next day, we hopped a cruise ship to the Bahamas to celebrate our honeymoon. We shared lots of love and lots of laughs, but our honeymoon phase was short-lived. It'd be a while before we'd experience the happily-ever-after part.

It took my new husband a little more than a year to leave the FBI, find a new federal law enforcement job, and join me back home in Seattle permanently. I didn't want to be a cheater anymore. I didn't want to have sex just to do it. I didn't want to party, drink, and smoke anymore. I wanted something different this time around. I wanted to be loving towards myself and faithful to my husband.

## A Wolf in Sheep's Clothing

All the therapy I had in the past was proving unsuccessful. Who could I talk to about removing this thorn from my side? A brilliant idea had occurred to me! I knew exactly who could help me kill this demon inside me once and for all. I remembered a pastor, who I hadn't seen in at least ten years, since the day my first husband walked out during the sermon because he felt the pastor was becoming a bit too political. I recalled how much wisdom and insight the pastor had. In fact, he was the pastor who baptized me. I rationalized that I didn't leave the church on my terms, but my ex-husband's.

I resolved that I would talk to the pastor. It brought a smile to my face and a sigh of relief as I thought about how he would help me figure out how to be alone and okay, find new hobbies, and discover a greater purpose for my existence. I researched the address for the church and was surprised to find that he had left the large congregation he once pastored and was now in a temporary location at a nearby high school. I began attendance. It felt good to be in the energy of praising and worshiping God! I quickly signed up to serve as a Sunday school teacher, and while my life was still in shambles, I was beginning to feel like the rebuilding was in full effect!

After attending a few services, I wanted to pay my respects to the pastor. Following one Sunday service, I filed into the line the church members would customarily form to thank the pastor for a great sermon and pay their respects as they exited the sanctuary. As I approached him, he looked at me and said with excitement and a big smile on his face, "Hey, my favorite couple!"

My shy and reserved response was, "Well, actually ... we aren't together anymore, and it's been a really tough transition for me." We shared a couple more words and as I proceeded to walk away, he blurted out his phone number in the presence of all the members behind me and told me to call him.

My number one goal was to remain focused and faithful until my new husband returned to Seattle. I called the pastor a few days later. We chatted a bit. I gave him the history about how my first marriage had ended and brought up how I felt my affairs were a by-product of unhealed wounds from my childhood. He didn't give me much feedback, only that he was sorry to hear that and we should meet up to discuss it further. Because he was in between churches, he asked that we meet at the local IHOP restaurant. In my naiveté, I agreed.

It was the day I was to meet with the pastor, a big and tall, burly, Melano man, chiseled and attractive on the pulpit, and I recall having internal dialogue with myself as I was getting dressed, "Don't do too much, you don't want to give the wrong impression. Girl, just throw on some flip-flops and jeans ... no need to get all cute." In alignment with my truest intention, I took care to dress with a certain level of modesty.

I arrived at IHOP, we greeted each other with a gentle hug, and proceeded to our table. I was mortified at what he would say just moments after we sat down. The first words out of his mouth were, "You are a sight for sore eyes." I knew by the look in his eye that this was not just an innocent compliment. I was disgusted, insulted, appalled, enraged, and intrigued all at once.

I sat in silence and absolute shock as he proceeded to tell me about his sexless marriage and how beautiful I was. I vacillated about whether to slap him and run or oblige his request for "just a massage" at my place. I was a deer in headlights. He had looked beyond my desire to heal and pierced me right at the thorn in my side.

He unapologetically persisted with his smooth talk, intellect, and pastoral prestige. The confusion I felt reminded me of when

I was around seven. My aunt's boyfriend at the time had a teenage son who I thought was very attractive. Truth be told, I had a crush on him. One day, my two other cousins and I were left home alone with him. He led me to the garage, pulled out his penis, and asked "Would you like to shake my friend Hank?" Intrigued, and afraid, I shook my head side-to-side with a shy grin. After asking me if I was sure a few times, he backed off with a simple response, "Okay."

If only the pastor had given up so easily ... After his repeated attempts at convincing me that it was *just a massage*, I made the regrettable decision to oblige his request. Following our IHOP dinner, we began to head towards our vehicles where he would follow me to the townhome I'd recently moved into. I was a mental, emotional wreck the entire drive! I kept thinking about how I should speed up, ditch him, and never speak to him again!

Fear, disgust, hopelessness, and lust where all present emotions. There I was, alone in my car, with a beast of a man following me. I was also drowning in loneliness, guilt, shame, and pain, and he was offering me my drug of choice—seduction. As much as I hated it, I chose the thing with which I was most familiar.

I was apprehensive and uncomfortable when we arrived at my place. My voice and my power to say no were taken away a long time ago. I felt completely on the hook. I was obligated. I had to perform. We proceeded to my bedroom, where I'd grant him his massage, using my inexperienced and unwilling hands.

We cuddled a bit, and I began to experience a multitude of emotions, including fascination for this powerful force of energy that lay by my side. All of it interrupted by the absolute agony I felt when the uninvited memory that I was *just married* entered my mind. We did not have sexual intercourse that night, but I did allow him to masturbate while taking in the curves of my body through the lamp of his eyes.

*"Your eye is a lamp that provides light for your body. When your eye is good, your whole body is filled with light. But when it is bad, your body is filled with darkness. Make sure that the light you think you have is not actually darkness."*
*~Luke 11:34-35 NLT*

Pandora's box had been opened, and there was no turning back. To pacify my loneliness, I developed a relationship with the pastor until my husband returned to reside with me permanently. Whenever we met up for the occasional dinner date, we'd have conversations about God and sex. I never really enjoyed the sex, but life had taught me that I was a performer, and sex was my act. I would make sure this was an act he'd never forget.

Truth be told, there were times when I hated him. I hated him for how he'd appear to be a sheep, only he was a wolf. I hated him for how he seemed to know exactly how to lure me in all of my weakness. I hated him for asking me to have sex in his private office just prior to delivering his amazing performance disguised as a sermon in the sanctuary. I hated that he was deceiving an entire congregation and that when it came to his sexual indecency, I was likely not the only one. More importantly, I hated myself for being willing to accommodate his request in the first place.

*"A Cherokee chief was explaining to a little boy, 'Each of us has two wolves inside, always fighting. One is the wolf of kindness, generosity, and love. The other is the wolf of selfishness, greed, and hatred. They are always at war.' The boy asks, 'and which one wins?' The chief smiled. 'The one you feed.'"*
*~Native American Proverb*

Who is this enemy that lives within me? How is it that I continue to do what I most assuredly do not want to do? I learned a few things from this experience. I learned that everyone has both a wolf and a sheep within them, and you become the sum of the one you feed the most.

I learned that if God could forgive the pastor, God could forgive me. I learned that a saint is just a sinner who fell down and got back up. I got to know the pastor with a certain degree of intimacy over the course of our affair. I learned that he was a broken man, looking for love in all the wrong places and faces, just like me.

## The Truth Will Set You Free

I never did have the ability to keep a secret for very long. The heaviness of secrets always tormented me right through to my bones. And this secret was heavy. I was a newlywed for Christ's sake! The pastor and I were about three months into our affair before I told my long-distance husband what was going on. And, just maybe, sort of, kind of, perhaps, I didn't tell the whole truth. I tried to downplay it by saying that the pastor and I were having more of an emotional relationship and that he was someone I could talk to as I adapted to being alone.

I was surprised by Eric's response. He was fairly okay with the situation as long as I could "keep it under control." (I would later find out that he was so open to the company I kept because he had a little temporary fix of his own.)

There I found myself again: sad, alone, and in a state of deep depression. I was sure that if I could just find a man I truly loved, my inappropriate behavior would end. I was sadly mistaken. Love *for* another was not enough to heal me. Love *from* another was not enough to heal me. In order to heal, I had to love myself.

I broke it off with the pastor and told him that my husband would be returning home soon and that I wanted nothing to be in the way of our building a good marriage. Two months prior to my husband's permanent relocation to Seattle, I travelled one last time to visit my husband near his job training facilities in Savannah, Georgia.

We were elated at the idea that there'd be no more monthly travel from one coast to another. As we sat along the waterfront, we observed a child happily at play. I turned to him and said, "Let's go back and 'do it,' and if it works, we'll name her Savannah." He smiled back at me in agreement, and we returned to our hotel. It was August 30th—my birthday. My flight home was scheduled for the very next morning. We only had one shot at love-making with the intention of baby-making.

Two weeks after my return home, I was met with morning sickness. Eric was thrilled to hear of my pregnancy! We were waiting excitedly for when we could determine the sex of our unborn child. It just had to be a girl! Her intended name was Savannah … George was simply not an option. Four months into my pregnancy, *she* was confirmed via ultrasound.

## Marital Conflict

When my husband Eric, whom I barely knew, finally joined me in Seattle, we were both surprised at what life together under the same roof looked like. He came home to a pregnant, cranky, judgmental, and vain woman, who was struggling with depression and self-loathing. Eric was happy and conflict-free. In fact, he worked so hard to avoid conflict that he simply did not communicate. Eric has always loved me. It didn't take him long, however, to stop liking me.

About four years into our marriage, Eric grew weary of supporting me through depression, the occasional affair, and the nasty custody battle for my son. Eric had been doing his best to stick around because, even through all that, he saw the light in me and felt my genuine love for God and my family.

I always strived to be a spiritual woman and a good wife and mother. I would set aside time to communicate and connect with my kids. I regularly prayed and sought God through the Bible, yoga, and meditation. I journaled, and I tried to be present for the needs of my home and my husband. I was also able to successfully manage a career in corporate leadership. There was just one *serious* glitch in my program.

## Straddling the Line

While on company trips, I would spend the daylight hours convincing my clients to do things my way, and with my external show of confidence and strong knowledge base about our products and services, they usually did. Evenings were a different story. After the obligatory client dinners, I would head back to my hotel, change into something a little more risqué, and head to the nearest lounge or nightclub. These were my opportunities to cop a feel of what life would have been like had I been single in my twenties.

I wanted to feel loved and valued. Unfortunately, I believed that my greatest value was my flesh. Rarely did these nights end with sex, but you best believe I straddled the line. This was the temporary high my flesh desired, but my spirit was never in agreement. I had a split mind. On the one hand, I knew that it was God's love and grace that had won my every victory. I knew that the light which shone through me was felt by others; the problem was that I was the one who doubted the true essence of my superpowers.

> *"A double minded man is unstable in all his ways."*
> *~James 1:8 KJV*

Thoughts of guilt, shame, and not-enough-ness spoke more loudly than anything. I knew logically that these thoughts were only figments of my imagination. My reality often didn't support those thoughts; yet, because I was thinking them, I believed them to be me, and I behaved accordingly.

The mood swings and marital conflicts were escalating. Eric and I were experiencing a sort of marital bi-polar disorder. One moment we were up, and it was all going to be okay. We were praying and healing together, and then the next moment would be filled with overwhelming grief, disappointment, and the hopeless feeling that there was no way to return our marriage to love.

We both agreed to let it all fall. We decided that the only way to save our relationship was to risk losing it all by giving ourselves what we thought we needed.

## Radical Self-Love

Eric needed peace. I needed an open relationship. We knew there was a possibility we wouldn't survive, but we could not be concerned with what the future might bring. Trying and failing was no longer an option. We had to jump off the ledge! For me, this was an act of what I call *"radical self-love."*

Radical self-love is when you give yourself permission to do the thing you have a burning desire to do, no matter whether it be considered good or bad. I caution you: If there are other parties involved who would be directly and emotionally impacted by your decisions, you should only engage in this process with their agreement. I asked my husband for his support in doing the *"unthinkable"* because I knew he would be impacted by my actions.

There are risks associated with radical self-love. When you take this path, you allow the *experience* to confirm what your spirit has probably been telling you all along. You will gain an affirmative answer on whether your desire supports you evolving by the very fruit you bear.

*"A good tree cannot bear bad fruit, and a bad tree cannot bear good fruit."~Matthew 7:18 NIV*

You might say that due to the high-risk, unknown variables, and the potential consequences of engaging in such radical actions, radical self-love isn't really self-love at all. While that would be a fair argument under normal circumstances, it is in moments of *insanity* that we believe pain is love and love is pain. It is in our insanity that radical self-love steps in and allows you to love yourself enough to give you what you *think* you need.

During one of my radical self-love moments of *insanity,* I met a fine, Persian young man. He was who you might fantasize about. He was nice, young, tall, handsome, and muscular. We met for coffee and lunch a few times before we decided to have a little fun. When we finally had sex, he had a nice package, but I felt no connection with the nicely decorated gift laying before me. I mostly performed. We had sex another time or two, and at the end of it all, I asked myself ... *for what?*

*"So I find this law at work: Although I want to do good, evil is right there with me. For in my inner being I delight in God's law; but I see another law at work in me, waging war against the law of my mind and making me a prisoner of the law of sin at work within me." ~Romans 7:21-23 NIV*

On another occasion, I reconnected with my old neighbor, Micah. Starting a new fling with him wasn't difficult to do. He lived not far from our new home and he would make it a point to drive to my neighborhood to walk the hill. I felt he would start up again like clockwork. About every three to six months it was like something in his spirit was driving him to make his presence known in a kind of silent offering. Over the years, I would ignore him—until I didn't.

One day, after seeing him on the hill through the windows of our local neighborhood Starbucks—where you could usually find me working while sipping on a *double-tall-extra-hot 'Cinnamon*

*Dolce' or 'Matcha Green Tea Latte'*—I lied and told myself I'd give him a call just to see how he was doing. Years had passed since our last fling. I convinced myself that this was all in innocence. We chatted over the phone, and Micah expressed the love he has always had for me.

He talked of how he knows we can't be together, but we should be friends. He insisted that we have lunch, and I finally gave in. The day I was to meet him I had so much nervous energy! Just like in the past, whenever I would head to meet him, I'd break out in a sweat, feel nauseous to my stomach, and have anxiety. And just like in the past ... I ignored my body's warning signs and proceeded anyway.

I remember hurrying to get my car open, and bam! The side corner of my driver's side door popped me in the lip! I knew that was God screaming at me saying "Don't go!" I tried to call Micah to get out of going, but he encouraged me, and I went anyway. There I sat, with half of my lip swollen, trying to look sexy from across the table. If that ain't insanity, I don't know what is!

After briefly experiencing what it felt like to be in an open relationship, I decided that sexual immorality was something I no longer desired. I became suicidal. I truly felt like I wanted to take my life because I couldn't figure out why I kept doing what felt like self-mutilation. My husband, who is a law enforcement officer, was always careful to lock his gun up in our safe.

I really don't believe I would have ever used it, but the truth is ... I thought about it. I would also think about veering my car right off the side of the large hill in my community. There was a time when I took more anti-depressant pills than I should have. I took them slowly. I truly did not want to overdose; I wanted to get attention.

At that time in my life, these actions were the only way I knew how to scream, "Somebody please help me!" It was in the depths of my lowest low that I felt the presence of God rush to my aid. It was when I ran full speed ahead and actually did the crazy things my mind told me I wanted to do that I knew I *never* wanted to do them again! When I sincerely decided to die to the flesh, God turned evil into good. This was my final act. It would be the most radical of all my performances. Act over. Curtains closed.

# PART 2: BAPTIZED BY FIRE

*"Beloved, do not be surprised at the fiery trial when it comes upon you to test you, as though something strange were happening to you. ~1 Peter 4:12 ESV*

# Chapter 5: An Abrupt Awakening

I was in my early thirties when God helped nudge along my desire to become new. It was just days before our daughter's fourth birthday. I had just picked her up from the Montessori school she'd been attending. I greeted her with love, buckled her up in her car seat, and proceeded towards home. As usual, I was filled with habitual nervous energy and in a rush to get nowhere.

Suddenly, out of the corner of my eye, I saw a car heading full speed ahead towards the front passenger side of my two-week-new car! I had nanoseconds to respond, and bang! Airbags inflated, smoke appeared, and haze followed. My audio sensory response muted. Everything was slow motion. It was as if I was abruptly jolted out of the reality of this world and projected into a realm of silence, clarity, and pure presence. I could sense everything going on around me with a keen hypervigilance.

I glanced over my right shoulder to make sure that my daughter was okay in the back seat. Next, I tried to get my car door open in an attempt to free us both from the smoke-filled vehicle. Panic threatened to overtake me when I realized my door was stuck. I knew I could show no signs of distress because she was watching my every move for her cues on how she should react.

I gave the door an intentional, forceful push, and, thankfully, it opened. I immediately went for the driver's side back door, reached in, whisked my daughter out of her car seat, and carried her to the nearest sidewalk. I assured her that she was okay and that accidents happen. Savannah handled it all quite well. She was shaken up a little, but I don't believe she cried. Thankfully, I was the one who took the brunt of the impact. She was unscathed.

I proceeded as per the normal protocol. I called my husband, filed a police report, and took down the other party's insurance information. When the officer arrived, he asked if I was okay. While I did feel some stiffness on the right side of my body, and particularly in my neck, I told him that I would be fine. I was more anxious to get my daughter home and out of that situation.

## A State of Dis-Ease

Over the next few days, my condition worsened. I began experiencing shoulder pain and tightness in my jaw and neck. My muscles began to ache as if every cell in that area of my body was filled with inflammation. The impact from the accident created such tight muscular constriction on the right side of my body that within a few months, I was diagnosed with Temporomandibular Joint Disorder, otherwise known as TMJ. If you know anything about this condition, you know it is no joke! It is still highly misunderstood and there is apparently no cure. I did not agree with the diagnosis. I knew that this was the manifestation of my soul's yearning for my spiritual awakening.

God is the Consciousness, which speaks to us in the *Still Small Voice*. It is when we do not hear the gentle, nurturing whispers that we get the inevitable scream. My abrupt awakening forced me to complete stillness. The ligaments in my neck and shoulders felt as though they were climbing up towards my head, wrapping tightly around my jaw bones, causing them to clench together. It didn't help that I was still healing from the dental work I had done to replace my silver fillings a few months prior to the accident.

I want to point out that I really didn't have to replace my fillings. The vanity within me wanted perfection which suddenly did not include the barely noticeable hint of silver fillings way in the back of my mouth interrupting my pearly whites ... Another moment of insanity. My bite was completely misaligned.

I could no longer hold lengthy conversations over the phone with my clients without feeling immense pain in my jaws, triggering a migraine or a newly developed lisp. I tried traveling a few times after developing this new disease and found that the effects of sitting in one position for hours at high altitudes only caused more tension, constriction, and severe tightening in my jaw, neck, and shoulders.

I refused to allow my doctor to prescribe pain medication. I had heard too many horror stories about prescription drugs and had a growing disdain for the pharmaceutical industry for leading our country down a deadly path. Nevertheless, the two doses of 800 milligram Ibuprofen per day my doctor prescribed was no match for what was going on in my body! I could not enjoy a good steak or anything else that required an even bite. Eventually, I ended up having to get a partial root canal on an otherwise healthy back tooth because it cracked in half while I was eating almonds.

It was extremely frustrating running from chiropractors to physical therapists to specialists. Nothing relieved the intense pain and discomfort. No one seemed to really know what was going on, let alone how to help me heal. I was beginning to believe that it was my running from doctor to doctor, constantly researching my condition, and worrying about getting enough work on the clock that was making me feel worse. It dawned on me that it was time I stopped seeking to heal through *medication* and started seeking my healing through *meditation.* I declare with praise and thanksgiving, "I am healed!" Let us call even those things that are not, as though they are. Yes, the faith of a mustard seed does have the power to move mountains.

*"Be still, and know that I am God..." ~Psalm 46:10 ESV*

## When God Calls, Answer

God was asking me to be still and take time to contemplate my life. I was ready to understand how I got here and how I could get to the life God wanted for me. I sought out my family doctor for a leave of absence approval. She agreed that I could not heal while working in my current condition and approved a nine-month leave of absence. This would mark the beginning of my metamorphosis out of the flesh and into the Spirit.

I spent most of the first few days of my leave crying out to God about the mess I had made. I realized, clear as day, how much my son still needed me and how unhealthy his father's living situation was. I realized how much my husband and daughter needed my presence. Sure, I was there physically, but my mind was often miles away. I realized how self-absorbed I had been for far too many years. I realized the disorder in my home and recognized that even my body could no longer sustain the disorder in my thoughts that gave birth to my actions.

One evening, as I sat in the sacred space I had created in front of the fireplace of my living room, tears streamed down my eyes like waterfalls. In a desperate and agonizing prayer, I cried out to God, "Everything the world taught me I am, I give to you ... Everything my life has taught me about women and the role we play in the world, I give to you ... I am empty now! You will have to show me who I am!" I was angry. I was frustrated. And I was ready for Jesus to take the wheel. In an instant, I felt completely empty of all self-identity. It was a scary feeling, but I knew it was an indication that God had heard my prayer.

With deep clarity, I heard God within me say, "*Evolve*."

I responded to the Voice inside my head, "What do you mean evolve? What does *evolve* have to do with anything?"

God replied, "If you are going to evolve, you must love yourself. If the world is going to evolve—it must love." The *Still*

*Small Voice* proceeded to say, "Look, the word *love* is coded within the word *evolve*."

There before me was a blank white board and a purple sharpie that my daughter had been using earlier that day for drawing. I eagerly picked up the marker and proceeded to write the word *evolve*. I underlined the first four letters, and there it was: *love*. As indicated within the following divinity code: we can only **evol**ve when we **love**, and whenever we love, we will most certainly evolve. Whoa! This was a powerful and defining moment that would change the trajectory of my entire life. This was the first of many *divinity codes* God would download into my being to share with you.

This deeply intimate encounter with God marks my very moment of transcendence. All at once, I was filled with a peace that surpassed all understanding. It was as if a light switch had been turned on inside of me. Over the course of the next few weeks, I continued to seek God's Will through constant prayer and meditation, and we continued our conversations. God spoke to me in impressions. It was as if there was a silent, yet very audible, communication going on inside of me, but from a space beyond my own intelligence.

When God called, I answered. I asked God for specific instructions on how I could evolve. I was instructed to create an organization called Evolve To Love. Love To Evolve®. I was instructed to devote my every waking moment to discovering what love really is. At the time, the term "Spiritual Advisor" was really uncommon; yet, that was the specific title I was given. I asked if I had to go to church, God's response was no. Little did I know, God would send the church to me. I asked if I had to change my dress code and dress like a nun or something, thankfully the answer was, "No, as I have called you, so shall you be. How will you reach my children if they cannot see themselves in you?"

Hallelujah was my response!

*"He has saved us and called us to a holy life—not because of anything we have done but because of his own purpose and grace. This grace was given to us in Christ Jesus before the beginning of time." ~2 Timothy 1:9 NIV*

I asked, "What about Jesus?"

God said as clear as day, "Jesus stays." In fact, I was directed to learn everything I could about love through the teachings of Jesus Christ, as found in The New Testament of the Bible. As I read the biblical accounts, I began to know a Jesus who did not really resemble the Jesus religion had taught me about. Sure, I had heard the scriptures before, but they came secondhand and fragmented. In addition to the study of Jesus, I was led to read the book of Proverbs for the practice of daily life principles. I affectionately refer to the book of Proverbs as PR-over-BS. This great body of text is primarily about true public relations over bull-sh*t.

I hope my occasional reference to a curse word does not offend you. If it does, allow me to remind you of this scripture to keep you with me on the journey to win the war between the flesh and the spirit:

*"Be not overly righteous, and do not make yourself too wise. Why should you destroy yourself? Be not overly wicked, neither be a fool. Why should you die before your time?"*
*~Ecclesiastes 7:16-17 ESV*

It was starting to become clear that I had been called to bridge the perceived gap between the secular and the sacred. Thankfully, my husband Eric would be the earth angel who would help me see it through. Just because God calls someone to your life doesn't mean your relationship with them will be a walk in the park. In fact, when it comes to your romantic relationship, God will likely choose someone who will show you yourself. Particularly the parts of you that you do not wish to see, from affairs to financial woes to all out thinking you are not going to make it. We have walked through fire to victory! Together we stand, with God as the center, having created a life filled with the fruit of the Spirit, which God promises us all who believe.

Eric and I did the work to evolve to love and keep our sexy sacred. For our tenth wedding anniversary, we renewed our wedding vows on a beautiful, clear, white sand beach in Jamaica. Like Moses and the Israelites, my forty days and forty nights in the wilderness had ended! I knew that my promised land was just on the horizon! I could taste the rainbow! I had no idea how it was going to happen, but I knew that somehow, someway, I would no longer live under the dark gray, water-filled clouds of Seattle by my fortieth birthday.

It was a miracle! Not one, but two Supervisory Federal Law Enforcement positions had become available in the Sunshine State of Florida! Each on opposite coasts, but I really didn't care which one. This sun goddess just wanted the sun! Eric interviewed for both positions. He was not chosen for the first, but he was hired for the second. We were elated to begin our relocation! The Lord as my witness, I moved to South Florida during the very month of my fortieth birthday!

As I was rummaging through our personal documents to ensure we had everything we needed for personal business, I ran across our original marriage certificate from our 7/07/07 Florida beach wedding and noticed that our wedding was officiated in the same exact county where we had just purchased our beautiful new home. God had brought our lives completely full circle!

It amazes me how God truly is a God of HEr word. The great symphony of our lives is orchestrated well beyond what we can begin to envision. Trust that with regard to your life, God has created the most classical melody. Then, be willing to fully surrender yourself to the flow of the Great Composer's baton.

Eric and I quickly began to understand that even before we were woven in our mother's wombs, God had called us to be a living witness that love does, in fact, cover all transgressions.

*"Above all, keep loving one another earnestly, since love covers a multitude of sins." ~1 Peter 4:8 ESV*

# Chapter 6: The Truth About Jesus

*"Thus it is written, The first man Adam became a living being; the last Adam became a life-giving spirit."*
*~1 Corinthians 15:45 NIV*

You were the children of Adam and Eve. Now you are children of the second Adam: Jesus. Jesus came so that the sins and consequences of Adam and Eve's fall could be dealt with once and for all. Jesus went up against all odds to teach us that when we reconcile ourselves back to love, we are not under the laws of death, destruction, and condemnation. You could say that prior to my awakening, I was a seductive, adulterous woman—or worse. I do not take offense. For all intents and purposes, those things were true.

Before you rush to judgment, however, let's not forget that I was also sexually abused, confused, broken-hearted, traumatized, and completely ignorant of a better way out. King David was once an adulterous murderer, Mary Magdalene was once an evil-doer, and Matthew was once a hated tax collector. All of them *evolved* to become some of God's greatest warriors for love!

Typically, we hear countless stories about the men of the bible: who they were and the great adversities they'd overcome before doing God's Will. The stories told about the women are often safe and sentimental, such as Jesus's Mother, Mary, and her immaculate conception, or Sarah who, because of her faith, was blessed to have a child with Abraham, even though she was thought to be barren and well beyond the opportune age for child-rearing.

What about the countless, messy stories of the adulterous women? As you read on, be mindful of the fact that in order for these women to have even committed adultery, there had to be willing men involved. In many churches around the world, you will hear very little, if anything at all, on the topic of sexuality and adultery. I know you might have your opinions, but WWJD (What Would Jesus Do)?

Let's look at how Jesus addressed these types of women.

## Case Study 1: The Samarian Woman at the Well

"Jesus said to her, 'Go, call your husband, and come here.' The woman answered him, 'I have no husband.' 'You are right when you say you have no husband. The fact is, you have had five husbands, and the man you now have is not your husband. What you have said is true.' The woman said to him, 'Sir, I perceive that you are a prophet.'" (John 4:16-19)

"So the woman left her water jar and went away into town and said to the people, 'Come, see a man who told me all that I ever did. Can this be the Christ?' They went out of the town and were coming to him." (John 4:28-30)

**Notice:** Jesus did not accuse the Samarian woman of anything. Can you imagine how much of a ruckus her personal life would have been and how many other lives she might have negatively impacted over the course of five husbands? And still ... No judgment? Jesus took a different approach. He simply restated the facts about her experiences.

Even more profound, rather than guilt-tripping her by focusing on her darkness, he took care to acknowledge her light by saying "You are right" and "What you have said is true." How did she respond to her encounter with Jesus? She drew more people unto him. I'd say that was a victory for the Heavenly Hosts!

## Case Study 2: The Woman Caught in Adultery

"The scribes and the Pharisees brought a woman who had been caught in adultery, and placing her in the midst they said to him, 'Teacher, this woman has been caught in the act of adultery. Now in the Law, Moses commanded us to stone such women. So what do you say?'" (John 8:3-5)

"And as they continued to ask him, he stood up and said to them, 'Let him who is without sin among you be the first to throw a stone at her.'" (John 8:7)

"Jesus said to her, 'Woman, where are they? Has no one condemned you?' She said, 'No one, Lord.' And Jesus said, 'Neither do I condemn you; go, and from now on sin no more.'" (John 8:10-11)

**Notice:** It was the *religious* scribes and Pharisees who tried to have the woman stoned to death. Jesus did not condone the stoning nor condemn the woman. He simply said, "… from now on sin no more." Jesus did, however, make a final address to the "holy men" saying: "You judge according to the flesh; I judge no one. Yet even if I do judge, my judgment is true, for it is not I alone who judge, but I and the Father who sent me." (John 8:15-16)

Pause here. This is a Selah moment. A praise and meditation moment. Did you catch that? Jesus judges no one. On the contrary, it is Satan who is referred to as the Accuser (Revelation 12:10). Whenever someone is constantly accusing you, that is a tell-tale sign of the master they serve.

## Case Study 3: Gomer, the Adulterous Wife

The book of Hosea is a story about Hosea's wife, Gomer. She was an adulterous woman whose journey reminds me very much of my own. She really thought she had that seduction thing down! The men she engaged with gave her some of the finest gifts. Her husband, Hosea, did not leave her; in fact, he pleaded for her to discontinue her behavior.

The Bible says she received strangers instead of her husband with her lewdness and whoring. God reminded her that it was actually Him who had given her bread, water, oil, and drink. Gomer eventually dealt with the natural consequences—or *karma*—for her actions and lost everything. Only at that point did she consider returning to her husband.

God did not smite Gomer or sentence her to death by stoning. What God did do is fascinating! God calls her back unto Himself by loving her while she was in the barren wilderness of the life she created.

> *"Therefore, behold, I will allure her,*
> *and bring her into the wilderness,*
> *and speak tenderly to her.*
> *And there I will give her her vineyards*
> *and make the Valley of Achor a door of hope.*
> *And there she shall answer as in the days of her youth,*
> *as at the time when she came out of the land of Egypt. And in*
> *that day, declares the Lord, you*
> *will call me 'My Husband,' and no longer will you call me 'My*
> *Baal.' For I will remove the*
> *names of the Baals from her mouth, and they shall be*
> *remembered by name no more."*
> *~Hosea 2:14-17*

Now some theologians will want to insert their intellect here by interjecting that the storyline in the book of Hosea is a metaphor for the fallen relationship between the Israelites and God due to their unfaithfulness and worship of false idols. I would absolutely agree. This actually further supports the point that how we function as individuals is a reflection of how we function collectively. Infidelity is infidelity whether it occurs individually, communally, corporately, nationally, internationally, or globally. Our public predicament is a reflection of our private lives.

I, just like these women, needed Jesus! I needed a spiritual intervention. I needed demons cast out of me. Thankfully, when I asked and *believed*, I received. I received a new way of understanding God. A God who was more concerned about my return home than my departure. A God who wanted to show me the power in my pain. A God who is not about rules and religion, but relationship. I have written *Keep Your Sexy Sacred* to share the thoughts of our Loving God with you, so you can also return home if you choose.

*"For my thoughts are not your thoughts, neither are your ways my ways, declares the LORD." ~Isaiah 55:8 ESV*

## God Turns Evil into Good

No matter how dark a room, the darkness diminishes instantly when introduced to the light. The same universal law applies to the darkness or *sin* within us. No matter how egregious the sin, truth and love will transmute it, for love *is* the light that shines away the darkness. But how can you heal what you do not reveal?

You might have been taught that love is a sentimental word reserved for romance. You may believe that if you open yourself to love, you will become someone's doormat. Chances are, this has already happened. Many religions unconsciously teach that you must dress a certain way, or follow certain sacraments, routines, and rituals in order to receive God's Love. But what if love could be found in all things if only you look for it? What if whenever you have fallen, your fall was not a falling backwards, but a falling forward—*if* you receive the love lesson?

Picture having a slingshot in your hand with a rock in the center. You pull back on the rock in the sling as far as you can, then simply let go to propel the rock towards your intended target. The further you pull back, the further the rock hurls forward. As I reflect with hindsight on my own falls and backslides, I can see the purposeful threads that were necessary for linking my experiences to my destiny.

Would it have been good for me to judge myself or begrudge my parents for not teaching me the value of education? How far in life would I have gotten if I held the limiting beliefs that I couldn't do this or that because I only received a formal education equivalent to that of a high school diploma?

I am crystal clear that it was God's intention to keep me from being indoctrinated in the viewpoints of this current system of thought in terms of what makes one *intelligent* or *successful*. No one can accredit these *Universal Laws of Love* to the thoughts of man. I cannot accredit them to myself. I know that without the activation of The Holy Spirit within me, these thoughts could not be formulated through me, nor delivered to you.

You are being called to enhance your Spiritual IQ®. Things change when you change the way you think about them. Allow God to show you the power in your pain, turn evil into good, and use your life as a light that illuminates Love's path for all to see.

*"Brothers and sisters, think of what you were when you were called. Not many of you were wise by human standards; not many were influential; not many were of noble birth. But God chose the foolish things of the world to shame the wise; God chose the weak things of the world to shame the strong."*
*~1 Corinthians 1:26-27*

## Turn on the Lights

Do not take offense when someone hurts you. God knew that you would experience what you went through. God knows every fear and pain, every disappointment and every victory! Imagine yourself as a child, afraid and alone in a dark room. There, on your dresser, you see a shape likened to a scary monster. You lay afraid and immobilized for a time with the covers pulled up to your eyes, imagining the terror of the boogie man.

In an instant, you decide to get up, turn on the lights, and voilà! It turned out to be just your favorite stuffed teddy bear or your jacket.

Now, apply this analogy to your fears, insecurities, and secrets. Which ones have been festering inside your gut, paralyzing you, stealing your mental well-being and your energy? Those things you have identified are the things you have kept hidden deep within yourself. The energy resides in the silence and hidden places, where the light of truth, transparency, and love cannot reach. Tell somebody, tell yourself, tell the truth—and be set free. Be the little child who decided to get up, turn on the lights, and shine the darkness of all illusions away.

*"For you are all children of light, children of the day. We are not of the night or of the darkness." ~1 Thessalonians 5:5 ESV*

## Die to Become New

When you decide to come into the light and walk in the Spirit, you will surely see a contrast between who the world taught you that you are and who God created you to be. Your moral compass will change, and you will find that what you once desired may have very well been killing you inside. You may even begin to feel pain in your body as your state of awareness brings you to the sobering truth about how your actions have impacted your vessel. You may experience very low energy due to the energetic blocks that exist in your body as a result of your former lifestyle.

The process of dying to the life you once knew will likely be painful. It was painful for me to see myself for who I had become. It was painful to clean out my closets, my pantry, my piles of paperwork filled with unfinished business. Even the colors of the paint on the walls in my home needed to change, and painting was a miserable process! While I absolutely loved the new hue of heavenly sky blue that graced the walls of my living room, I decided I would leave painting to the experts from then on out!

There were countless goodwill bags, filled with fine clothing, jewelry, and other "stuff," which only served to cover up or disguise myself from the ugliness I felt inside. The worst part of dying to my old self was how it forced me to see how much damage I'd done to my marriage and how I was not present enough with my children. My family needed me, and it was agonizing to face the truth that I had not been there.

I asked my husband and children to forgive me. I asked Jesus to teach me how to forgive myself, and with sweat and tears, I committed to cleaning up the mess I had made. I hated my former life. I lived in Seattle at the time, and while some people thrive there, the gray atmosphere more than two hundred days per year was wreaking havoc on my energy and my mind! It often hurt just to put one foot in front of the other as I walked up my staircase during the winter months.

I was tempted to believe I had Fibromyalgia, Raynaud's disease, or some other undiagnosed health condition. Admittedly, I had become a bit of a hypochondriac. I scheduled my fair share of doctor's appointments, and the doctors kept finding nothing. I finally surrendered everything to God and decided that I was more than just fine. I was in optimal health! I resolved that the environment didn't suit my genetic makeup. I needed more sun by virtue of my very design, and I would be in a new environment soon enough.

I surrendered to the pain. I pressed through the guilt and shame. I meditated, prayed, cried, cooked, cleaned, and, more often, I rested. Deconstructing my old self and reconstructing my new self was not easy to do. That's putting it lightly! Each day felt like I was dying to live. But better to die to live than to live a life so miserable that, in the end, you simply lived to die.

*"Anyone who loves their life will lose it, while anyone who hates their life in this world will keep it for eternal life."*
*~John 12:25 NIV*

## No Affiliations

The most difficult thing for me to die to was my attachment to the spirit of sadness and depression caused by the fundamental feeling that I was just *not good enough*. It was very difficult for me to go against the grain of my thoughts. To combat this little problem, I decided that regardless of what my mind and body felt like, I would seek God anyway. I could have no affiliations with the lies I once told myself about my worth.

The more I studied the scriptures, the more I would die to the Jesus of my religion and be reborn to a Jesus who was not only non-religious, but my brother, who was always there to hand me flowers whenever it rained ... Even when I was the one who had caused the storms.

Here are just a few examples of how Jesus was about relationship over religion:

- Jesus healed on the Sabbath day (work was forbidden on this day by Jewish law).

- Jesus did not accuse the women caught in adultery.

95

- Jesus got angry and flipped over the tables in the Temple.

- Jesus drank wine, danced at the party, and hung out among "sinners."

- Jesus said those who serve God are his mothers, brothers, and cousins.

  o He had no bias in loyalty to blood family over spiritual family.

- Jesus allowed himself to be anointed with the oil and tears of a sinful woman.

  o "'Therefore, I tell you, her sins, which are many, are forgiven—for she loved much. But he who is forgiven little, loves little.' And he said to her, 'Your sins are forgiven.' Then those who were at table with him began to say among themselves, 'Who is this, who even forgives sins?' And he said to the woman, 'Your faith has saved you; go in peace.'" (Luke 7:47-5)

- The Bible describes Jesus as being unattractive to the naked eye.

  o "Jesus grew up like a young plant, and like a root out of dry ground; he had no form or majesty that we should look at him, and no beauty that we should desire him." (Isaiah 53:2)

  o It is important to point out that Satan was created externally beautiful and his vanity caused his fall. It was Jesus who was truly beautiful in God's sight.

- What may be most difficult to believe is that Jesus gave you permission to embrace and acknowledge scientists, sages, and prophets like Quan Yin, Buddha, Swami

Yogananda, and other healers of our world, whose missions were to show us the way to love. No biblical scripture more eloquently proves this true than the following:

*"John answered, 'Master, we saw someone casting out demons in your name, and we tried to stop him, because he does not follow with us.' But Jesus said to him, 'Do not stop him, for the one who is not against you is for you.'" ~Luke 9:49-50 ESV*

Did Jesus just acknowledge that another man, who had *no affiliations* with him, had the ability to cast out demons? Sure, this may be taught in religion. But are you being taught that such a powerful, superhuman person, is you?

If this bumps up against your religious beliefs, I encourage you to stop. Take a deep breath and allow God to breathe new life, new wisdom, and new understanding into your soul. Or would you choose your religion over the very words of Jesus Christ? Remember, it was also Jesus who said:

*"I tell you the truth, anyone who believes in me will do the same works I have done, and even greater works, because I am going to be with the Father." ~John 14:12 NLT*

## Truth vs. Illusion

I trust that you are feeling the liberating and perhaps slightly uncomfortable reality that your prior understanding of God and Jesus may not have been crystal clear. Count it all joy that life begins at the end of your comfort zone.

"Is this degree of confusion and deception really so difficult to fathom when we know that Satan is the temporary ruler of this world?" (John 14:30) Our adversary and his legion disguise themselves as angels of light. Would it be so farfetched to consider that Satan also hid himself in many world religions? It was, in fact, religious law that hung Jesus on the cross.

*"And in his teaching he said, 'Beware of the scribes, who like to walk around in long robes and like greetings in the marketplaces and have the best seats in the synagogues and the places of honor at feasts, who devour widows' houses and for a pretense make long prayers. They will receive the greater condemnation.'" ~Mark 12:38-40 ESV*

Thankfully, Jesus is no longer on the cross. He lives again. When Jesus died, he took with him the power of sin and death. He made void the consequences of Adam and he himself became the second Adam, our new Founding Father. This time around, the rules are short and sweet. The quality of your entire life is in direct proportion to how much you love.

*"'Teacher, which is the great commandment in the Law?' And [Jesus] said to him, 'You shall love the Lord your God with all your heart and with all your soul and with all your mind. This is the great and first commandment. And a second is like it: You shall love your neighbor as yourself.'" ~Matthew 22:36-39 ESV*

Sounds simple enough. But then why is it so difficult for us to get this love thing down? In the next chapter, we'll explore what religion *without* relationship has taught us about love.

# Chapter 7: Religiosity vs. Relationship

*"If you claim to be religious but don't control your tongue, you are fooling yourself, and your religion is worthless. Pure and genuine religion in the sight of God the Father means caring for orphans and widows in their distress and refusing to let the world corrupt you." ~James 1:26-27 NLT*

With all the theologians, pastors, priests, elders, deacons, and many other men of the pulpit running our world religions, how could the connection between sex and the original sin be overlooked?

Why aren't sermons that address issues such as adultery, sex trafficking, child abuse, rape, molestation, and pedophilia being preached in most churches? Those seeking healing from these trespasses of the soul are sitting in the pews wondering why nobody is addressing their specific needs.

A lot is being said, but how much are the members really being spoken to? We can no longer underestimate the one who comes pretending to be an angel of light, but is, in fact, darkness. This is a love offering, an olive branch, delivered by the white dove with a message: "Peace. Be still and know—there is a difference between religion and relationship. Allow God's plan to unfold not outside of, but *through* you."

*"'For I know the plans I have for you,' declares the LORD, 'plans to prosper you and not to harm you, plans to give you hope and a future.'" ~Jeremiah 29:11 NIV*

For me, and I am certain many others, religion was a necessary pathway on the journey to God. There are some amazingly progressive churches out there, for which I am personally grateful. There is also a dark side existing within religion *without relationship* that we must expose to the light. Let's take this opportunity to engage in observation without condemnation.

In alignment with my intention to deprogram you of illusions, I will bring to your attention the reasons for religion's inability to have any real and lasting impact on the collective consciousness of our world. Why take the risk of raising such a taboo topic? Because we will not change what we are unwilling to acknowledge.

Ask yourself, what is the goal of religion? Obvious answers might be: to help its followers find a personal relationship with God, to teach humans how to love one another, or to help people heal from emotional pain. The truth is, a divorce rate of nearly 60 percent gives no grace to those in the Christian faith. One in four young girls is being molested and sex trafficking is one of the fastest-growing organized crimes in the world as a multi-billion-dollar international industry.

The long-standing conflict between the Israelites and the Palestinians is rooted in religious indifference, and Sunday is the most segregated day of the week in America. We can conclude that the intended goals of religion are far from being met.

**Here's the story of Michelle, a Caucasian woman who grew up very "religious," but the fruit of the spirit was nowhere to be found:**

I remember coming home from high school to my very angry mother, who had been told by some secret person who she would not divulge, that my best friend Kathy and I were hanging out with "black boys."

Yes, it was true. Their names were Jerry and Timmy, and they were extremely kind, considerate, smart, ambitious, honest young men. Straight-A students on the basketball team—involved in extracurricular activities and not involved in drugs or alcohol. The kind of boys your parents normally would be proud that you were associating with. Which was why I was so confused about the level of anger my mother had about these boys who she had never met and knew nothing about.

Truth be told, my friend Kathy and I did not see color and we enjoyed their company and wanted to have a relationship with them and, yes, we had even shared a kiss or two with them.

My mother went on to tell me that I was forbidden to talk to, date, or have any type of romantic relationship with a black boy because it was not accepted in our society and I would have a very hard life if I were to do this.

My reply was "I can't believe you. You make me go to church three times a week and learn about the unconditional love that Jesus taught, but yet you're telling me that because of the color of someone's skin, I should not love or like them? That's not what Jesus taught. He said love your neighbor as yourself. You're such a hypocrite!"

I was slapped in the face, sent to my room, and told I was on restriction for an indefinite period of time.

It was an unfortunate defining moment in my life because, after that, the "white boys" I dated were not high-quality like Jerry and Timmy. They ended up being users, losers, and abusers for both myself and my best friend. My life would have been much better if I had gone on to have a relationship with one of those upstanding young men, but I had other lessons to learn and journeys to take.

*"'These people honor me with their lips, but their hearts are far from me. They worship me in vain; their teachings are merely human rules.'" ~Matthew 15:8 NIV*

## The Fallacies of Religiosity

Have you ever engaged in conversation with someone who was trying to pitch you their religion? Does the conversation go great as long as it flows in the direction of their beliefs, but the moment you bring up a taboo topic like abortion, sex before marriage, or sexual orientation, the conversation quickly becomes quite awkward?

In my biblical studies, I have found that what the Bible actually instructs us to do and what much of religion teaches are all too often vastly different things. Let's revisit the idea that Jesus said, *"you are all gods" (Psalm 82:6)*. If we believe what Jesus said is true, then why do many religious folks in most predominant faiths scoff at people who call themselves a god or goddess? You yourself may have felt a twinge of fear at the thought of seeing yourself in this light; yet, this *is* the light you are.

Many doctrines do not delve into the scientific or metaphysical implications of what it means to be a "god," and this is the beginning of the error. How can you understand the God within when mainstream religion teaches of a God out there? Jesus was bold enough to call himself God, and religious men had him executed for blasphemy.

The issue is not the sacred scrolls; the issue is man's regurgitation of misinformation, calling it God's law. I share these scriptures with you standing solely on the solid ground of the power these words carry. This is your opportunity to look again and decide for yourself what these words mean to you. I trust that your own internal guide—The Holy Spirit within you—will give you wisdom and understanding.

There are several Christian denominations that claim to follow Jesus whose core message is love and non-judgment. So why is it that so many people feel so judged when they fall outside of their prescribed religion's man-made laws?

*"But the Holy Spirit produces this kind of fruit in our lives: love, joy, peace, patience, kindness, goodness, faithfulness, gentleness, and self-control. There is no law against these things!" ~Galatians 5:22 NLT*

All scrolls and literatures rooted in love should be taken into consideration when seeking to understand God. These books are gifts to aid us in evolving, and we can expect that God knows how vastly different we all are. It is reasonable to believe that SHe has created different pathways to HEr; nevertheless, love is the thread that binds them all because God is love.

From Christians to Catholics, Mormons to Sikhs, agnostics, and in between, as a Spiritual Advisor, I have had the honor of successfully guiding people from many walks of faith to a deeper relationship with God. My clients have all given me deep insight into both the gifts and the fallacies of their religions.

While many of my clients' religious practices serve them well in some way, I am always astounded and honored by their reports of how much more closely they walk with God and how much more clearly they can see God working in every aspect of their lives. The fruit of our labor of love is undeniable.

Let us collectively analyze the fruit religiosity has produced and respond with a sense of urgency to what we see. Are you a part of your church staff, choir, or clergy? What does the energy frequency feel like? Are you a pastor, deacon, elder, sister, brother, or someone else with influence at your place of worship? Are you a member? What does *your* energy frequency feel like when you think about the interactions, circumstances, and goings-on in your life?

Test the fruit. If the fruit is good for the tasting, by all means, do not change a thing. If the fruit is foul in any way, don't bite it! Is God calling you to cut off old branches, throw them in the fire, plant new seeds, and bear new fruit?

*"If anyone does not abide in me he is thrown away like a branch and withers; and the branches are gathered, thrown into the fire, and burned. If you abide in me, and my words abide in you, ask whatever you wish, and it will be done for you."*
*~John 15:6-7 ESV*

## One Body with Many Members

*"For the body does not consist of one member but of many. If the foot should say, 'Because I am not a hand, I do not belong to the body,' that would not make it any less a part of the body. And if the ear should say, 'Because I am not an eye, I do not belong to the body,' that would not make it any less a part of the body. If the whole body were an eye, where would be the sense of hearing? If the whole body were an ear, where would be the sense of smell? But as it is, God arranged the members in the body, each one of them, as he chose. If all were a single member, where would the body be? As it is, there are many parts, yet one body. The eye cannot say to the hand, 'I have no need of you,' nor again the head to the feet, 'I have no need of you.' On the contrary, the parts of the body that seem to be weaker are indispensable, and on those parts of the body that we think less honorable we bestow the greater honor, and our unpresentable parts are treated with greater modesty, which our more presentable parts do not require. But God has so composed the body, giving greater honor to the part that lacked it, that there may be no division in the body, but that the members may have the same care for one another. If one member suffers, all suffer together; if one member is honored, all rejoice together." ~1 Corinthians 12:14-26*

How backwards is it then for us not to acknowledge the gifts of God within everyone—every faith, every culture, every tradition—where love is their aim? A common tactic used to

104

divide the Body of Christ (*the human race*) is to add some sort of religious law to the mix to invalidate another person's efforts towards their own enlightenment.

No, it is not love to assert your religion on another person as if you know better than they do; what it is they need for their own salvation. This is the very judgment Jesus instructed us not to do. A lighthouse doesn't run around the ocean looking for ships to save. It simply shines its light, and the ships seeking its refuge inevitably find it.

*"For no one can ever be made right with God by doing what the law commands. The law simply shows us how sinful we are."*
*~Romans 3:20 NLT*

## Closets of the Men of the Cloth

*"Dear brothers and sisters, not many of you should become teachers in the church, for we who teach will be judged more strictly." ~James 3:1 NLT*

The sexual abuse of boys and other parishioners in the Catholic Church is a moral crisis and a spiritual catastrophe.

A recent *USA Today* article tells a far too common story about a priest, Reverand David Poulson of Pennsylvania, who, in addition to being accused of many heinous acts, admitted to being "aroused" while tutoring a boy, hugging him, and sharing sexually suggestive text messages with multiple boys. The Diocese knew of Poulson's sexual predator tendencies but did nothing to report him to authorities for several years—and only then in response to a Grand Jury subpoena.

According to the grand jury's presentment, which has been made public:

- Poulson sexually assaulted one victim repeatedly in church rectories at St. Michael's Catholic Church in Fryburg and Saint Anthony of Padua Catholic Church in Cambridge Springs. The abuse at the rectories usually happened on Sundays—after this victim served as an altar boy at Mass. These assaults took place more than twenty times.

- Poulson required this victim to make confession in church and confess to the sexual assaults to Poulson, who served as the priest receiving the boy's confession.

- Poulson also assaulted this victim and a second victim at a remote hunting cabin that he owned with a friend in Jefferson County. The cabin was off-the-grid, ten minutes off the main road in a rural location. It lacked electricity, heat, or running water. Poulson would bring the youths to the cabin, watch horror movies with them on his laptop, and then assault them.

Poulson's case is an example of how abuse and cover-up continue to plague the Catholic Church. The church has vowed to reform and has paid billions of dollars of parishioners' tithes to victims. In Pennsylvania, Poulson was one of the 301 predator priests identified in a sweeping Grand Jury report that detailed child sexual abuse in six Pennsylvania Catholic Diocese and religious leaders' efforts to cover it up. The investigation identified more than 1,000 victims.

Another recent sex scandal reveals that twelve Catholic priests who served in Arkansas were accused in another investigation over sex abuse allegations. The charges date back to the 1960's. It was reported that eight of the twelve priests have already died.

I don't know about you, but I am seeing a trend when it comes to the rape and molestation of "boys" in the Catholic church. And there are cases where it happens to women and girls as well. We can no longer overlook the repeated patterns of not only sexual immorality, but also the prevalent homosexuality within the hearts and minds of the Catholic priests, especially considering their religion is adamantly against homosexuality.

What programming are these priests receiving and regurgitating as part of their doctrine that would cause this level of insanity to become so widespread? Since we know that we are in a war of spirits and principalities, we can conclude there are demons behind this. How did they make it in? Through which earthly vessels did they experience themselves? Demons have no power beyond the power we give them.

## Two-Faced Men

It deeply saddened me to discover that the pastor I knew on the pulpit was very different from the pastor I would come to know privately. During my reluctant affair with the persuasive pastor of the Christian Baptist church, I took note of how he not only wanted to have sex but wanted to have sex in the sanctuary.

On multiple occasions, he would ask me to meet him in his office before the Sunday morning services. I once obliged his request. It was very sobering to sit in the pews watching him preach a sermon, while the congregation jumped up and down, shouting and praising in reverence to this *man of God*.

I am not judging. I am simply stating the facts. Another fact is that I allowed myself to have an affair with him. A few years after I had broken it off, we had a brief and polite exchange in communication via social media.

The pastor asked to meet me for coffee, and I believed that with all we'd been through, he would know engaging in a sexual relationship was not an option. We were cordial when we met. He flirted a bit, and our brief conversation ended. I was uncomfortable. I thought that was that. I felt regret for even engaging him again, but I was glad it was over.

He had other ideas. He started sending me private messages about how I knew I wanted him. Now far enough in my personal walk with God, I knew better, and I told my husband, Eric. We agreed to call the pastor's wife. We invited her over to our home where I would tell her everything.

My husband and I were absolutely shocked to encounter a woman with a very blank demeanor about her. It seemed as though she was hollow inside. Her response, "I have been telling him if he wants to leave, he can go." Her presence was cold and numb. I felt very strongly that the pastor had backed her into corners like this before.

If you have been sexually abused in the church, tell your truth. Shine a light on the darkness so that you can begin your healing journey. As for the men or women who have hurt you, give them to God. Do not be attached to what their consequences may or may not be. Your act of forgiveness has nothing to do with them and everything to do with your own freedom.

*"If we confess our sins, he is faithful and just to forgive us our sins and to cleanse us from all unrighteousness."*
*~1 John1:9 ESV*

Violence, rape, sex trafficking, child marriage, and all manner of sexually immoral behaviors impact far too many women and children worldwide. This is a global epidemic and a direct slap in God's face. India is known as a country of great spiritual enlightenment; yet, it has one of the highest percentages of heinous rape crimes in the world.

In India, a woman is reportedly raped every fifteen minutes and a victim of a crime every two minutes. In an attempt to manage the issue, India's government increased punishment for rape of an adult to twenty years in prison and approved the death penalty for people convicted of raping children under the age of twelve.

Our progressive United States is at the top of the list of usual suspects who engage in rampant sexual deviancy against women and children, but no country is immune. The numbers are woeful. Every year, over 17,000 children are taken in the US and sold into trafficking. **Forty-six children are taken every single day from our own backyards.** We have a responsibility to address the defamation of the feminine energy of God. Why isn't the mission towards healing the global epidemic of demonic sexual deviancy a top priority of our great world religions?

**Here's the story of a woman named Ann. She faithfully attended the same church for twenty-five years only to uncover a wolf in sheep's clothing:**

One of the most surprising relationships I had was with the minister of my church. He was an extremely handsome man with a muscular physique and was also a dynamic and powerful speaker. I attended his church for twenty-five years, sitting in the front row every Sunday. I learned so much from him on my spiritual path. I considered him my spiritual mentor.

Over the years, I became more involved in the church, teaching classes and running the bookstore, and I started to get to know the minister behind closed doors. Like many other men I knew, he talked about the opposite sex and did a little flirting. From the conversations we had, you would not have thought he was a minister. At first, I was surprised by some of these conversations, but it always seemed like light-hearted fun. My minister was married to a beautiful woman and had adult children and grandchildren.

Looking back, I can see now that he was *grooming* me to take advantage of me sexually. He made small gestures over a long period of time, moving the line further and further. I found him to be very attractive, but I was not going to cross the line by having an affair with this married man.

One Sunday, I was working in the bookstore at church and just about everyone had gone home. He came over to me and my friend (who he also joked around with) and gave me a hug. Then he said, "I need to teach you about level two and level three hugs." I quickly replied that I wasn't interested in those types of hugs … even though I had no idea what he meant specifically. I knew it was about getting closer to me or touching me inappropriately. He said I needed to trust him.

About a month later, I was talking to him after church about needing some business photos. In addition to being a marketing and sales professor at the local college, he had his own photography business. He said he would be happy to take the photos at no charge in his home studio. We set up a day and time and I didn't think much about it. When I got to his house on the appointed day, I asked him where his wife was, and he said she was working. So here we were, alone in his house.

We went to the basement and he showed me some places outside the house and in his studio where we could take the photos. I went into the bathroom and put on my first change of clothing. He took dozens of photographs of me. We were having fun and joking around as usual. I thought the photoshoot was over and he said he wanted to do some *risqué* photos of me just for fun, so I would have them for my own personal records and use.

I asked him what he meant, and he pulled out a portfolio of several women dressed in sexy lingerie and some were practically naked. I guess the term that comes to mind is *boudoir* photos. I told him I really didn't need photos like that since I was single, but he insisted we take a few.

My gut was telling me not to do it, but he was very persuasive. He had me take down the straps of my shirt and open my legs and he even wanted me to pull my skirt up to my waist, which I declined. I was becoming increasingly uncomfortable and told him I had to go.

After this incident, I felt guilty that I had brought this on by my occasional flirting and being nice to him, but also by not setting clear boundaries with him. I thought it was my fault that he had come onto me.

I continued to attend church and felt uncomfortable about talking to him privately, so I tried to avoid him. One day he said that his wife was going out of town and we should get together. I said okay, but I didn't really plan on meeting with him after the uncomfortable and inappropriate photoshoot.

He began calling my cell phone, which he had never done before, and insisting we meet. I told him this was inappropriate since he was a married man and that I was not going to have an affair with him. He said I didn't understand things and he needed to teach me. He also said his wife didn't care. I was trying very hard to be clear that nothing was ever happening between us. He said, "You know you want me, too."

After two or three such calls, I told him I wasn't speaking to him anymore and that he should never, ever call me again. He acted like I didn't just say that and continued to move on his agenda. I refused to answer his calls after this. In fact, I stopped going to that church and never went back. I often wondered why some women suddenly disappeared from the church. Now I understood.

Having worked in the legal field for seventeen years, there is something known as a fiduciary relationship, which basically means a relationship in which one party places special trust, confidence, and reliance in and is influenced by another who has a fiduciary duty to act for the benefit of the party.

I trusted him as my minister and spiritual mentor in what I deemed a fiduciary relationship. Unfortunately, I trusted him blindly because of his position in the church. I did not follow my intuition and gut that were telling me things were moving in the wrong direction and were very inappropriate. I wanted his acceptance and friendship, so I overlooked many of his behaviors.

## A Global Warning

The root cause for the heartache and pain in our world is clearly the devil's disdain for the feminine energy of God. The time is now for *you* to take a stand with the God of love who is both feminine and masculine. The woman is the missing piece of the puzzle for world peace. I have come with a double-edged sword to send a clear and confident message in the authority of the Holy Spirt within me: **"Cease and desist the pillage and plunder of women, children, and nations. It is *game over* for life as you have known it."**

*"For the word of God is living and active, sharper than any two-edged sword, piercing to the division of soul and of spirit, of joints and of marrow, and discerning the thoughts and intentions of the heart." ~Hebrews 4:12 ESV*

## Intimacy with God

It is only your personal relationship and experience of God that will cause you to become fully aligned with the virtues and vibrations of love. And your relationship with God is exactly that—*yours*.

While there is nothing wrong with having an anointed yogi, teacher, pastor, priest, or rabbi who is well studied give you guidance, it is more important that you take responsibility to see for yourself through the clear lens of your own internal knowing.

How often are you taking in the living word of God for yourself? I work with my clients for a finite amount of time, usually six months to two years, because it is my goal to align them not to my beliefs, but to their own internal guide. The Holy Spirit within you will show you your own way. If religion is the path set for you, Amen! If yoga and meditation is the path for you, Namaste. Just remember, the tree is ever and always known not so much by where it is planted, but by its fruit.

*"But the wisdom from above is first pure, then peaceable, gentle, open to reason, full of mercy and good fruits, impartial and sincere." ~James 3:17 ESV*

Wouldn't you love a more intimate and *uncomplicated* relationship with God? It is written, "God is not a God of confusion." (1 Corinthians 14:33) Allow *KYSS* to be the beginning of your transcendent spiritual journey out of the flesh and into the Spirit. When you see, you cannot un-see. When you know, you cannot un-know. In fact, deep-seated within your soul, you already know. I am here to simply guide you to *re-member*. Yes, rejoin as an integral member of the One-Body we all together were created to be.

*"But the Advocate, the Holy Spirit, whom the Father will send in my name, will teach you all things and will remind you of everything I have said to you." ~John 14:26 NIV*

As I reflect on my journey to a deeper understanding of God, which began as a child through the teachings of the Jehovah's Witnesses, I question how a doctrine could be so anticipatory for what they call the "New Order," when everything and everyone is perfect and you never die. You just grow old, then younger again. Moving in such a direction sounds interesting, but the thought that who we are now is the sum of one, big, huge mistake never sat well with me.

Early-adopted religious beliefs can cause us to live much of our lives feeling as though something is inherently wrong with us. For me, that included our entire world. I felt I had no permission to enjoy this life—that it'd actually be a sin to do so.

The Jehovah's Witnesses emphatically teach that theirs is the "one true religion" and that there is no hell. I will say, I have witnessed firsthand the living hell that became the lives of those who failed to adhere to the rules of the doctrine. Topping the list were my mother and the first of my two younger brothers.

I have seen the deep programming and traumatic spiritual and emotional implications of *"ours is the only way"* doctrines. The idea of those who have been disbanded or dis-fellow-shipped seeking another pathway to God—is usually frowned upon and even dismissed as a viable option. If the true aim of religion is to teach the power of love, it would be a good idea to apply the *Universal Laws of Love*, namely: " ... **love *does not* insist on its own way** ... " (1 Corinthians 13:5).

Instead of doctrines rooted in "thou shalt not's," I wonder what would happen if more religious leaders were more like Jesus and actually delivered messaging from the perspective of "thou shall"? For example, "You shall do whatever you shall." You are made in the image and likeness of God. You have the power to create. This free will is your birthright. Know that love is the solid foundation on which your world was created and the universe is self-correcting. Whatever your actions are, there will be an effect. However you are affected—good or bad—is a result of the universe allowing exactly what is necessary to bring about the balance of love. The choice is yours. Choose wisely.

*"So then each of us will give an account of ourselves to God."*
*~Romans 14:12 ESV*

On the topic of "thou shalt not's," many mainstream religions frown upon the use of alcohol and smoking—both man-made substances. Understandably, anything that does not give health and life brings one closer to death and destruction. But there's a deeper rabbit hole. Many world religions are also adamantly against the ingestion of natural plant medicines like Cannabis and Ayahuasca. In the next chapter, we'll explore whether this stance is rooted in truth or ignorance.

# PART 3: IN THE SPIRIT

*"But I say, walk by the Spirit, and you will not gratify the desires of the flesh." ~Galatians 5:16 ESV*

# Chapter 8: The Power of Plant Medicines

*"Then God said, 'I give you every seed-bearing plant on the face of the whole earth and every tree that has fruit with seed in it. They will be yours for food.'" ~Genesis 1:29 NIV*

You cannot bear fruit without branches. You cannot have trees without seeds. These green giants of nature receive their intelligence directly from the sun through a process called photosynthesis. Plants convert the light of the sun into the energy humans and animals need to function optimally in life. You need not look far to find a study on the immense overall health benefits of a plant-based diet. Have you ever stopped to think about why God created an earth so vastly green?

*Could it be that natural plants are gifts from God, not just here to sustain us physically, but also spiritually? Are trees, in fact, the carriers of the Breath of God, which was breathed into all humankind at the beginning of time? The oxygen we receive from trees keeps us alive. In turn, we provide trees with the carbon dioxide they need to thrive. Right at the basic, most fundamental level of our existence, humans and plants have a symbiotic relationship. If Mother Nature is not God, then who is SHe?*

Trees, plants, flowers, mushrooms, and all sorts of nature's beautiful botany receive their *super-food-power* directly from the light of the sun. Imagine that God were the Sun and you were a sunray. The sun cannot exist without naturally creating its rays, nor could the sunray exist without having the sun as its Creator. To the naked eye, the sun and the rays appear separate (there seems to be space between them), but they are—and can only ever be—one and the same.

Do not underestimate the power of the sun. King Herod went on a rampage to kill every firstborn boy under two years of age because he knew that Jesus had been born. How did he know? He saw his *star,* or "sun" in the east. Like Jesus, we all might have the energy of a universal star connected to us.

Just as King Herod was on a mission to blot out the Great Son from our world, there are modern-day King Herods who do not want humanity to discover the miracle in plant medicines, which also receive their natural intelligence from the direct light of the sun. Could it be they fear they'll lose their monetary fortunes with our spiritual awakening?

In 2014, total pharmaceutical revenues worldwide exceeded one trillion US dollars. You would think that given the massive amounts of money made by pharmaceutical companies, more lives would be saved. The truth is much bleaker than these companies would like to make public. The rates of death by way of overdose are disheartening! Just how many of these dollars make no sense? Let's explore further.

## The Case for Cannabis

More than two million Americans are suffering from opioid addiction. More than one hundred Americans die each day via opioid overdose that started with synthetic prescription drugs. I wonder what would happen if we did some scientific research on the health of church-going, devout, religious folks? What would their medicine cabinets look like? Would this be in alignment with God's promises for those of us who serve the Lord?

*"A joyful heart is good medicine, but a crushed spirit dries up the bones" ~Proverbs 17:22 ESV*

These man-made drugs usually serve, not very effectively, to suppress symptoms of disease which we know are usually brought on by being in a constant state of *emotional stress* or *"dis-ease."* I don't know about you, but I would not be looking to suppress my symptoms, I would want to address their underlying causes using the wisdom of spiritual insight and, if necessary, the assistance of organic, plant-based medicines—all while substantially reducing risk from the long list of side effects that come along with ingestion of manufactured drugs.

CNN's award-winning chief medical correspondent, Dr. Sanjay Gupta, conducted a CNN special report entitled simply *"Weed."* His findings were jaw-dropping. Before marijuana was banned in the 1970's, it was used in cough medicines and to treat more serious disorders like leprosy and epilepsy, both diseases that were prevalent in biblical times.

Marijuana is proving quite effective in the treatment of adults and children who suffer from seizures, cancers, and other acute medical conditions. If you were the parent of such a child, would you consider a plant-based, holistic approach if you knew it would rid your child of violent shaking spells or intense nausea and enhance their quality of living?

Just as Jesus taught us when he turned water into wine at the wedding party or asked us to drink the wine in remembrance of the blood he shed for us, all things should be done with reverence, respect, and in moderation. I was first introduced to marijuana in my teens. My first husband and I would smoke daily before we quit cold turkey after seven years of smoking together.

While under its effects, we'd have deep conversations about God, get the munchies (a slang word for food cravings), and would also get really lethargic at times. In hindsight, we had no respect for the plant, and he consumed it much more excessively. About once a year or so, Anthony would have a recurring bipolar episode.

If you've ever experienced someone with bipolar disorder, it is one of the scariest things to witness from the outside looking in. While in the grips of his episodes, he didn't seem to be afraid of much of anything. I feared for his life! I witnessed him walk to the neighbor lady's house in his underwear and t-shirt asking to use the phone. When she declined, he dragged her around her house. I begged her not to press charges, and because she knew who he was outside of this episode, she agreed not to do so.

At other times, he'd rant and rave about the "end times" while walking throughout the neighborhood with a deliberate sense of urgency, yet with no concern for the surrounding cars or buses. He also exhibited hypersexual behaviors. The most personally traumatic of his episodes for me was when he carried our fully-clothed, two-year-old son into the shower, expressing with urgency that demons were trying to get him and he had to wash them away.

I called 911 that night and specifically informed them that he needed an ambulance and medical attention. The police showed up instead and arrested him. That was the last thing he needed and the last thing I wanted. I knew that this was not him. When he wasn't in an episode, he had his issues, but, in general, was a kind person. I picked him up after a few days in jail and was absolutely devastated to find that he had been badly beaten and bruised by the police officers.

I believe that was the last time he smoked weed. Although marijuana never had such an adverse effect on me, I quit with him to support him and our son. Anthony never did have another episode that I know of, and he also stopped taking Lithium, the drug prescribed by his doctor that caused him to blow up like a balloon amid other side effects like confusion and incoherence.

Marijuana is not for everyone, and respect and moderation is an absolute must! It's really no different than the casual, once-or-twice-a-month glass of wine drinker versus the one who drinks multiple times a day. One has an addiction while the other is experiencing health benefits.

It would be more than a decade before I tried weed again. It was almost a year after my awakening car accident when I realized that I was not getting better. In fact, my symptoms had worsened. My neck, back, and shoulders were in a constant state of tension, pain, and discomfort. I would have daily migraines and was beginning to develop a speech impediment due to the tight pull on the ligaments in my jaw.

My doctor suggested a prescription of Vicodin, but my instincts told me to refuse, just like I refused to take the Oxycodone my doctor offered me after the birth of my daughter. But the 800 milligrams of ibuprofen I took twice daily had virtually no effect, and I was starting to become more concerned with what the little, white, powder-packed pill was doing to my stomach lining!

I grew weary of seeking the next remedy, all while my condition was getting worse. That's around the time Dr. Sanjay Gupta's special "Weed" aired on CNN. After watching the countless benefits and personal stories of children and adults who were able to get their lives back after marijuana, I was convinced that I should give it another try. At the time, I lived in Seattle, Washington, also known as the "Evergreen State" for its lush green trees which grace the landscape—a progressive place when it comes to the use of cannabis.

The legalization of marijuana is gaining quite the momentum. It is currently legal for either medicinal or recreational use in over half of the United States. Within weeks, I made an appointment to qualify for my official medical marijuana card. This time, I was legit! This time, I had reverence and respect for the plant. Admittedly, I still struggled with thoughts of guilt. Although I wasn't practicing my religion of origin, the dogma still ran amuck in my mind, constantly seeking an opportunity to remind me that I was doing something wrong.

I ignored the accusing devil on my shoulder and practiced radical self-love. I prayed and asked God to show me whether or not weed was good for me by way of the fruit. I remember the first puff I took in my upstairs master bathroom. I sat on the rim of our oversized tub with my face as close as possible to the open, screen-enclosed window. With the first inhale and exhale, I could literally feel my muscles and ligaments release and let go of the tight grip they seemed to have on my bones! Months and months of ibuprofen *never* did that!

Marijuana was a tremendous help in relieving my chronic pain and discomfort. I didn't need much and I didn't consume much. As little as a quarter gram or a pea-sized ball of the green leaf twice a day was just what the doctor ordered! Weed was so good to me that when my condition improved drastically—and it did—I quit taking it as part of my daily regimen.

Marijuana isn't a *highly* addictive drug, but it can be addictive. As with most things in life, discipline and moderation are key. The Drug Policy Alliance (DPA) explains, "Fewer than 10 percent of those who try marijuana ever end up meeting the clinical criteria for dependence, whereas 32 percent of tobacco users and 15 percent of alcohol users do."

Let's take a look at the alarming statistics on the use of and addiction to prescription drugs.

More people report using controlled prescription drugs than cocaine, heroin, and methamphetamine combined. Most abused prescription drugs fall under four categories, based on the number of people who misuse the drug:

- Painkillers: 3.3 million users
- Tranquilizers: 2 million users

- Stimulants: 1.7 million users

- Sedatives: 0.5 million users

With regard to addressing the best approach to healing our bodies and minds, we know that pharmaceuticals and other synthetic drugs are causing addiction and death at disproportionately high rates compared to marijuana and other plant medicines. *Fox News* integrative alternative medicine TV personality and columnist Chris Kilham wrote in a *New York Times* article, "People in the U.S. are more cranked up on pharmaceutical drugs than any other culture in the world today. I want people using safer medicine. And that means plant medicine."

## The Spirit in the Plant

*"God is spirit, and those who worship him must worship in spirit and truth." ~John 4:24 ESV*

There are several spiritual thought leaders today who support the use of plant medicines. In a documentary film (which I highly recommend you watch) called *The Reality of Truth* written by Mike "Zappy" Zapolin, Spiritual Advisor and Author Deepak Chopra points out that our brains have receptors to these plants because we have the same nature. Is there a possibility that we can access the Kingdom of Heaven *before* we actually die? Could plant medicines assist us along the way?

Deepak goes on to say that the gift such plant medicines have is their ability to cause humans to break away from the illusion of separation and enter the reality of truth. When Deepak was asked by Zappy what we can do to solve the world's problems of hunger, social injustice, global warming, war, and all other causes of insanity, Deepak's response was: "Let's have a party."

I wonder how quickly our world would change if we all sat in the Amazon forest and drank these spiritually healing plant medicines.

Another unsuspected and fascinating miracle of God took place as a result of Zappy's decision to create this life-changing documentary. Gerard (Gerry) Powell, a good friend of Zappy's, generously loaned Zappy his home for the interview with Deepak. Gerry took what he heard during the interview very seriously and went to Costa Rica to ingest a plant medicine called Iboga. Iboga is a psychoactive indole alkaloid derived from the rootbark of an African plant: Tabernanthe iboga. It has been increasingly noted for its ability to treat both synthetic drug and alcohol addiction.

Gerry's life was an absolute mess prior to his Iboga experience. He had plenty of problems that his wealth couldn't cure. Gerry smoked and drank excessively, he had unhealthy relationships with women, and he had a big ego. After just one plant ceremony, Gerry was a completely changed man. His closest friends and family noticed a difference in Gerry's disposition immediately upon his return!

Gerry reported that while in ceremony—or what I call "the Spirit of the plant"—he received specific instruction from the feminine Mrs. Moon. She took Gerry through a series of events, including visions of his childhood, revealing to him the root of all of his problems, which began when he was sexually molested by his grandfather at just three years of age. While in the plant medicine, Gerry went through a process of forgiveness and Mrs. Moon gave Gerry a new heart.

Mrs. Moon proceeded to instruct Gerry to go to Costa Rica, buy property, and make a plant-based healing center. The Moon told him what building to buy, how much to buy it for, and how to treat his spouse and children. Gerry did just as he was instructed and created "Rythmia Life Advancement Centers," a retreat where people can go to expand their consciousness and heal themselves with plant medicines as an optional healing modality.

Michael Bernard Beckwith, New Thought Leader and Founder of the progressive Agape International Spiritual Center, has written a curriculum specifically designed for Rythmia, called "The Answer is You."

*"And God said, 'Let the earth sprout vegetation, plants yielding seed, and fruit trees bearing fruit in which is their seed, each according to its kind, on the earth.' And it was so."*
*~Genesis 1:11 ESV*

## My Miracle in the Medicine

Five years into my journey of spiritual awakening, my life was truly blessed. All around me, I could see good fruit. I could see the Kingdom of Heaven in our midst. My relationships with my husband and children were blessed. I was healing the lives of thousands of individuals who were seeking spiritual solutions to their problems.

God blessed us with a beautiful home in sunny Florida, situated along a glorious river, which gently flows daily. I often sit in gratitude on my living room floor, stretching, while in awe of the light of the sun which reflects off the water. The beautiful natural wildlife and heavenly cloud formations provide an exquisite experience of God's Magnificence every day!

Sure, things weren't always 100 percent perfect. Moving across country nearly swallowed the available balances on our credit card accounts. Our son, Martin, was transitioning to life on his own as a young adult. We were buying new furniture, painting, decorating, and the vast number of other things that come along with such a major life transition. Still, there are worse problems in the world. We truly did have the desires of our hearts.

There was one problem: I felt a deep disconnect between my reality and how I actually felt inside. I was growing weary in the spirit. From the moment of my *divine download*, I knew I was to create a very unorthodox organization which would serve to help God's children see life through new lenses. I witnessed the power of the work in the individuals I served, and I longed to serve on a greater scale.

Each day, I would press to find that next door that God would have me walk through to expand this new way of understanding God. While some doors were opened, many were dead ends, and others were downright slammed shut in my face!

I was tired of the sweat and tears associated with entrepreneurship. I was growing weary of having created something so transformative; yet, I didn't fully understand its greater purpose. Why did God give me these gifts? Who am I called to serve? Specifically, *how* am I called to serve them? I needed a word from God for what was next.

One evening, while standing outside, gazing at the beautiful, universal stars from my backyard, I began praying, "God, I know you're using me to do your will, but I still feel the pain of a broken heart. I don't know what it is. I cannot put my finger on it. Help me … Please. Jesus! You're going to have to show me something. Give me a clue of what you're doing here." I was frustrated. I felt like giving up but knew I couldn't. I'd come too far. I'd witnessed the good fruit of my work in the lives of too many to just up and quit. But I needed God to let me in on HEr plans for my life.

Two years prior to this moment, I was watching an online subscription television program called GAIA. I ran across a documentary on plant medicine, specifically Ayahuasca. I was very intrigued by the plant, and thought to myself, I'd love to do a spiritual ceremony someday. I dismissed it because I knew that I wasn't going to South America any time in the near future.

Back to the prayer in my backyard. After the prayer, I decided to find some enlightening programming to watch in an effort to guard my mind and keep me in the right spirit. As I was searching GAIA for what to watch, a "suggested program" popped up and caught my attention. It was another documentary about Ayahuasca.

Watching the program reminded me of how interested I had been in partaking of this plant medicine. I decided to hop online and search for places that facilitate the plant ceremonies legally. And what do you know? God moved me just two and a half hours away from "Aya!" *Soul Quest Ayahuasca Church of Mother Earth* is legally authorized to administer the plant medicine and, in fact, has facilitated thousands of ceremonies to date.

Indigenous peoples from South America to North Africa have been using plant medicines as far back as 2000 BCE and very likely since the beginning of time. Cultures that do ingest these plant medicines as part of their sacred spiritual ceremonies tend to have greater qualities of peace, love, and unity among them— qualities which are lacking in other more modernized societies.

It is plausible to believe that God has given us these plants to help us penetrate more deeply into the vortex of the complex, yet brilliant, network of neurons in our brains.

I talked it over with my husband and he was in complete support of my decision to partake in an Ayahuasca plant ceremony. He said that he felt it was just the breakthrough I needed, and he gifted me with a spiritual plant medicine weekend retreat for our eleventh wedding anniversary. It all happened so fast! I was scheduled to ingest Aya within just two weeks! You remember my old friend, fear? It reared its ugly head again!

I began thinking thoughts like: What if I have an undiagnosed medical condition that causes me to die after ingesting Aya? How could I even take such a risk like this of leaving my family and children? What are people going to say when they find out the "spiritually enlightened" founder of Evolve To Love® is no longer with us because she did a "drug" and overdosed?

When I shared these thoughts with my husband, he continued to reassure me that this was the next step in my journey to understanding more about how God is using my life. Truthfully, no other option seemed viable to me.

The day had arrived when I was to partake of the plant medicine. There I sat in my car, outside my home in the driveway, suitcase packed and in my trunk. I was overwhelmed by fear and anxiety. I called my husband and he encouraged me to proceed. He told me that if I felt discomfort with the situation when I arrived, I could simply turn around and walk right back out the doors I'd just entered. I resolved that this was it! This was the only way I was going to learn more about this Great Manager I'd been working for but didn't really understand.

I began my two-and-a-half-hour commute. The fewer the miles, the closer the storms. There was a torrential downpour! The usually turquoise Florida skies were dark, gray, saturated, and heavy. The roaring thunder and lightning cracked and boomed as if the entire universe was angry! I was swimming in a sea of fear and uncertainty. All the while, I knew I had to do it.

Everything I'd discovered in my research told me that this is what God had called me to, and my life was in HEr hands. In the midst of the storm, I had an epiphany. *This is what it means to die to become new.* You must confront every fear and terror of your mind and face even death, just as Jesus did on the cross. You must be willing to die to become new.

*"Even though I walk through the valley of the shadow of death, I will fear no evil, for you are with me; your rod and your staff, they comfort me." ~Psalm 23:4 ESV*

I was reminded all at once that God was with me and that many humans do not answer God's calling because we are unwilling to die to the things we love, to our fears, and even to beliefs that do not serve us. I resolved that I was willing to give up everything I loved, including my family, my children, and even my sanity. What if Ayahuasca had an adverse effect on my brain and I would never be the same? Yes, I had to die to that thought too.

It was six o'clock in the evening when I arrived at the *Soul Quest* spiritual retreat center. A few other members were already there. Other participants filed in slowly as the evening progressed. The newbies like me were all nice and cordial with one another, but you could definitely feel the twinge of tension and fear in the air! The volunteers were lovely people. They were kind, gentle, and reassuring.

The opening ceremony was scheduled to begin at ten o'clock that night. We would spend the few hours we had to spare getting acclimated to the environment and each other. We were given a tour of the facilities and an overview of the ceremony—what to do, what not to do, what to expect, what not to expect. We also did some really calming and centering breath work.

Each of us was given an opportunity to choose from one of the several covered cots that lay about the lawn of the backyard. I chose the cot nearest the edge of the awning. I wanted to be certain I could look up at the heavenly stars and receive the support of the Universe while on this trip into the unknown. As the volunteers handed out the plant brew, they instructed us on how to consume the medicine.

Carlos approached my cot with a bright smile filled with love as he handed me a small Dixie cup filled with just two tablespoons of Ayahuasca. Carlos instructed me to drink it, then pour a little water into the cup and swish it around to be sure to get all of the medicine. Of course, I did not do that. I drank one of the two tablespoons and placed the thick, brown, prune-juice-tasting concoction down beside me.

We were told that it could take up to an hour for the plant's medicine to become active, and that activation usually occurs following a purge by way of vomiting or diarrhea. There I lay, in a peaceful, surrendered, and meditative state, gazing at the clouds in the sky. Thankfully, it had stopped raining. The sun had gone down, and there was a warm and gentle breeze.

Thirty minutes in, and I felt nothing. I heard God say, "Did you follow the instructions or are you in the same fear that you came here to get rid of?" Reluctantly, I grabbed the cup and drank the remaining tablespoon. I sat the cup down and laid back down.

After another fifteen minutes had passed, I heard God again, "Are you completely following the prescription as prescribed by Carlos?" I took a deep, fully surrendered sigh, picked up the small cup again, poured my water in, swished it around, and drank. See God, happy now?

It is clear why people don't get addicted to "Aya." No one wants to do a "drug" that will likely make you sick, throw up, or have diarrhea before it takes effect. And depending on how much healing work you have or have not done prior to ingesting the plant, you may or may not be able to handle what the Spirit in the plant will cause you to see. "Aya" meets us right where we are, giving us not always what we want, but always what we need.

An hour and fifteen minutes in and I felt the purge coming on. The volunteers had left little white buckets at the foot of our cots. Mine sat there, awaiting my inevitable visit. I proceeded to vomit. This was unlike any other vomit I'd had before. There wasn't really any solid content; it was more of a brown, watery consistency. Surprisingly, there was something about throwing up while in this process that actually felt good. Cleansing. After the brief but intense meeting with sickness, I lay back down on my cot and gazed up at the illuminous night sky.

## The Visions Begin

I was a little afraid. I was also very much in the power of the medicine. I knew there was no way out, so I allowed myself to be present with it. My first vision scared me. Off in the distance, I saw the silhouette of three trees that looked like the shadows of three big monster faces arguing. I heard God say, "See something different." Suddenly, they looked like three trees who were just chatting.

These *Tree-pals* were hugging by way of their branches and leaves touching, as they appeared to be chatting about the good ole' days—laughing like three Amigos, merely by way of the shapes they formed together. By now I was beginning to feel very comfortable and fully surrendered to the medicine. I was open to whatever "Aya" wanted to reveal to me.

The clouds above me had literally changed form before my eyes. The first form I saw was likened to the shadow of a skeleton head. I observed it without judgment and decided I would not be afraid. Then the cloud transformed into what looked like a baby cat or baby lion's head. I was like, whoa! This is a trip! Are the clouds actually changing form before my eyes?

Perhaps plant medicines like Ayahuasca were responsible for the strange visions and prophesies the prophets received as written in the book of Revelation, which speak of dragons, demons, angels, and all types of "hybrid creatures" fighting the war between heaven and earth.

*"Then I saw another mighty angel coming down from heaven,
wrapped in a cloud, with a rainbow over his head, and his face
was like the sun, and his legs like pillars of fire. He had a little
scroll open in his hand. And he set his right foot on the sea, and
his left foot on the land, and called out with a loud voice, like a
lion roaring." ~Revelation 10:1-3*

Thankfully, my visions and experiences ranged from absolutely magnificent to … palatable. It all felt as real as real. At the same time, I knew cognitively that I was having a *hallucination*. I also felt that it was very much okay. This is how powerful God is. SHe can move Heaven and Earth for you and conspire with the birds, stars, clouds, trees, and the breeze to give you such personal attention that you believe you are HEr only child.

*"But ask the beasts, and they will teach you;
the birds of the heavens, and they will tell you;
or the bushes of the earth, and they will teach you;
and the fish of the sea will declare to you.
Who among all these does not know
that the hand of the Lord has done this?
In his hand is the life of every living thing
and the breath of all mankind."
~Job 12:7-10 ESV*

As I continued to watch the clouds, the baby lion took on the likeness of an adult male lion's head. It looked very much like the head and big bushy mane of Simba's dad, Mufasa, from *The Lion King*. Those visions soon vanished. In all of this, I was very cognizant of my surroundings. I could see, sense, and hear other people in their own personal process.

Some were groaning in agony, some crying, while others were blissfully dancing. Through my eyes, everyone began to look pixelated. I was in a very peculiar space within two realities. And with all that was going on, I could still get up and walk myself to the bathroom.

When I closed my eyes, I could see the most beautiful and vivid of repeated patterns. It was as if there were a kaleidoscope inside my inner eyelids. At one point, the shapes began to look as though they would form a big, black snake. I spoke to Aya in my head and said, "If you want to show me a snake, I will see it." Thankfully, I never did see a full-on snake.

Other times I felt as though I was traveling through some sort of vortex, like a deep black hole by which I would travel through the dimensions of space and time. Again, I told "Aya," "I am willing to see what's on the other side." "Aya" never took me to the other side. Perhaps I was not ready to see.

Nevertheless, I was done with the light show. I was ready to get the love lessons I'd come for. I asked the plant to show me any darkness left within me and to show me anyone I have not fully forgiven. Aya's response was very soft yet authoritative, "We will do that tomorrow. Tonight, I am going to fill you with the pure joy you never experienced as a child." In an instant, my entire body became flooded with an indescribable dose of serotonin and dopamine—or happy-happy joy-joy to put it in simple terms!

My feel-good receptors were completely activated. I was starting to become very relaxed in my experience. I said to Mother Aya, "Tell me about Enrique" (the name I affectionately call my husband, Eric). I received another, very unexpected surge of "giddy." I had never, ever experienced such pure joy in my life! Absolute bliss pulsed through my entire being, from my head to my toes!

The Spirit in the plant really cracked me up when I asked HEr about Jesus. The answer was very much something along these lines, "You know … Mother's love all their children, and don't have any favorites, but ... *he was my first.*" I was completely connected with Her sense of humor as SHe told this facetious joke!

Much of the time, I was elated for no apparent reason. At times, I had to draw the covers over my head so as not to interfere with the experiences of those around me. Imagine a child rolling around on the bed, giggling uncontrollably as you tickle her. That joy, bliss, and innocence you see. That was me on my cot outside on the lawn in that majestic midnight. In between the laughter were very distinct and specific messages about my childhood experiences. I assure you, this was not just a "high." I received many *revelations* and answers to questions which greatly assisted me on my journey towards forgiveness and self-love.

## The Answers Come

While the pure joy remained, the laughter was interrupted by an extremely itchy and irritated middle finger. I asked the medicine why my finger was so itchy and uncomfortable. HEr response, "Your daughter's finger is just fine. She is a composer of music, put her back in piano lessons."

A little backstory is necessary for this to make sense. When my daughter Savannah was about two and a half, I received a phone call from her childcare. The voice on the other line opened the conversation by saying, "You need to pick up Savannah and she is definitely going to need stitches."

I was done in! Who calls a parent and says this? I hung up the phone and rushed to the childcare center where I found my little Savvy seated on the table in the office and visibly shaken. She had a dingy looking rag wrapped around her left hand. The childcare director told me that Savannah was playing in the playground near a gate and "someone" rushed by, swung the gate open, and sliced her finger. They offered to pay any and all medical expenses, but couldn't say who caused the accident. We suspected it was one of the staff members.

I rushed Savannah to the nearest emergency room. When the doctor was ready to take a look, I asked my precious baby girl to look away as they unraveled the rag to reveal the traumatizing sight of the tip of her middle finger, severed and dangling by a mere thread of skin. The doctor's response, "We can't help you; you have to take her to Children's Hospital."

I contacted my husband Eric to inform him of what had happened. He left the office immediately and headed toward the hospital to meet me. I was devastated! Sure, I was praying the whole time and holding onto the faith of a teeny tiny mustard seed! I really thought my daughter was going to lose the tip of her finger. I tried my best to maintain my composure around her. When we arrived at Children's Hospital, the doctor informed us that they would be attempting to stitch her finger back together; however, they couldn't guarantee there wouldn't be any nerve damage.

Our daughter lay on the operating table and fought like a champ! She resisted the process until they sedated her. Savannah persisted to kick her feet wildly in the air until she and her little legs gave way and dropped with a thud back down on to the operating table. She was out and so was I.

The whole situation was too much for me. I had to go outside to get some fresh air while Eric stayed with our baby girl. The doctors stitched and wrapped her up, and we were on our way. Savannah healed completely over time.

We enrolled Savannah in piano lessons from the time she was four years old until she was seven. She was eight years old when we relocated across country. Although she hadn't played piano in over a year, we decided to bring the beautiful baby grand we were given as a gift to our new home. It is true what they say. The best things in life are free.

While in the medicine, I was instructed to put Savannah back in piano lessons. Aya told me that particular finger was the strongest of all her fingers. It gives her just the edge she needs! I obeyed Aya's suggestion and enrolled Savannah in private piano lessons within weeks of my return home. She absolutely loves her piano lessons.

After I received and acknowledged the message, my finger stopped bothering me completely.

## The Sting of Our Circumstances

Suddenly, the left side of my mouth felt irritated, slightly swollen, and painful. I have never been stung by a bee, but if I could imagine what a bee sting feels like, this would be it! I asked Mother Aya, "What is this about with my lip?"

SHe replied, "When he slapped you, it really hurt." SHe caused me to remember a time when I was ten years old.

I was playing with two boys who lived around the corner from my grandparent's house. We were probably doing things we should not have been doing, but nothing sexual. The two boys walked me back to my grandparent's house, I rang the doorbell, stepped back beside the two boys, and waited. My grandfather opened the door, looked at the boys, then at me with a piercing stare. Out of nowhere, he slapped me hard right across my face!

My grandfather came to me while I was in the medicine and asked for forgiveness. I forgave him. He also told me that he was the reason my mother drinks, to tell her that he is sorry and to ask her to forgive him. I did relay this message to my mom. When this experience came to a close, unlike my finger, my lip still hurt, so I asked, "Why does my lip still hurt?"

HEr reply, "When *he* slapped you, it really hurt."

Aya took me to another experience when I was slapped at fourteen years old. This man was in his twenties. I was young, fast, and naïve. He was an islander, who I had met at a reggae club. We exchanged numbers and chatted the next day. I was engaged in a very brief stint with modeling at the time and asked him to take me to a nearby college where they were shooting a movie in which I was cast as an extra. It seemed to take forever and a day to play one of many people in a large crowd filing into the stadium for a game. The night ended late, at around two o-clock in the morning.

He picked me up when it was all over. Instead of taking me home, he took me back to his place, a converted garage in the back of his mildly popular reggae artist friend's home. He began trying to have sex with me on his pull-out bed. I resisted. I wasn't very attracted to him. In fact, certain aspects of his demeanor repulsed me.

I got squeamish and started telling him no. My lack of cooperation ended abruptly with a swift, sharp, stinging slap dead across my face! My whole body became limp with resignation. I was being date raped. I allowed him to have his way with me. We had missionary sex, and while I hated the wetness of the slimy kisses, the penetration from his penis felt really good. Another thing to add to my quickly crowding wall of shame.

We woke up the next day as if nothing had happened. He took me home, called me again, and we went out several more times over the next year and a half. I was suddenly in an abusive relationship. I was practically living with a man who had beaten me on several occasions. I was a victim of domestic violence.

He once beat me so badly underneath a freeway overpass that I played dead. He drove me to a nearby hospital emergency room, crying and screaming about how sorry he was, and he stayed by my side the entire time. When the doctors examined me, I could not muster up the courage to tell anyone that he had beaten me. I returned to my abuser's home that same day.

Our relationship came to a screeching halt when I got pregnant at fifteen. This was not my first pregnancy. I was twelve or thirteen when I got pregnant the first time, within months of having my first period. My mother does not recall this ever happening.

According to my recollection, when my mother learned of my pregnancy, I was immediately taken to a nearby abortion clinic. There was no talk of right or wrong or any other implications for my actions. There was only a resounding and unspoken message: *you will not be with child.* Period. End of discussion.

I was completely numb to the impact the experience had on my soul. By now, I'd learned to numb the sadness within my inner being by giving pleasure to my outer being.

I moved in with the abuser and became pregnant shortly thereafter. He'd do the usual cooking, cleaning, and giving me his version of love, which was more like obsession and possession. One day, when I was four months pregnant and starting to show, he came home laughing hysterically. When I asked him what was so funny, he said he'd gone to visit his two-year-old daughter, who I knew he had, but he never mentioned her much. He continued to tell me how her mother was "tripping" and how they got into a fight (of course, I knew what that meant).

He laughed and grinned the whole time as he told me about his baby girl following behind him and her mother while picking up the braids that were falling (better yet, being yanked) out of her hair. The image was terrifying! I saw that woman as me and that child as mine. In the blink of an eye, I saw myself trapped in a life of domestic abuse. How could he think it was funny? I thought, "If I stay here, this will be the death of me. I cannot bring life into this life."

The very next day, I found my way to a clinic my mother had taken me to for checkups a few times in the past. I remembered the doctor's name, Dr. Chavez. When I arrived at the front counter, I asked for Dr. Chavez. I explained that I did not know anything about my insurance and that I was in an abusive relationship with a man who raped me. I asked for an emergency abortion. They obliged. The very next day I called my mother, asked for a plane ticket, and boarded a flight to Seattle. I never spoke to the abuser again.

Mother Aya wanted me to know that when these men slapped me in the face, they not only abused me, but also knocked my dignity, my confidence, and my self-esteem out of me. During this sacred ceremony, Mother Aya would return it all, with more on reserve! Do not underestimate the sting of the circumstances life has put you through. That pain needs your attention. In order to heal, you must tend to your wounds.

Forgiveness is a necessary stop along the journey to healing. My abuser was sexually abused by his mother's housekeeper when he was a young child. I forgave him for not knowing how to heal from his pain. He was a hurt person, hurting other people. We were mirror reflections of each other's unhealed places.

After a few more indescribably beautiful love lessons, I resumed my blissful laughter and expressions of deep gratitude as I lay under the starry night sky. I was so content with my first plant medicine ceremony that I did not want to consume the plant medicine again. Then I recalled when Mother Aya said she would show me my darkness during the next day's ceremony. I would be an obedient child.

## Ceremony Day Two

The next day began with a group integration session in which everyone spoke of their experiences from the night before. Afterwards, those of us partaking in the daytime ceremony got situated outside on our mats, underneath a beautiful network of trees that seemed to work together to create a nurturing canopy. I was directly in the center. I could look up and see the sun perfectly placed in the hole that peeked through the canopy's top. I felt like a baby being held in the womb of the trees.

We did yoga and other breath work to prepare us before we ingested our two-tablespoon dosage. About forty-five minutes passed before I entered the grips of the medicine. Aya told me that I was a sun goddess and that today would be my welcoming ceremony into my work for the Queendom. Ironically, the song entitled "Sun Goddess" by the popular 1970's music band *Earth Wind and Fire* has always been a favorite of mine!

Unlike the night before, the nausea I felt on this day was overwhelming. I wanted to purge so badly, but couldn't. I kept assuming the position by getting on all fours and hovering over my white purge bucket, but nothing. Aya told me that I would not purge so I decided to go with it and breathe in whatever Aya wanted me to feel. I quickly discovered that every time I felt nauseated, someone around me would vomit. I was feeling a deep and profound oneness with the emotional energy of everyone in the ceremony.

I began to receive the love lesson Mother Aya was offering me. God wanted me to understand that my gift to the world was my ability to feel and address the wounds of many. I needed to know that I could handle it. I could hold it, I could sit in it, I could help heal it, and it would not consume nor overtake me.

I danced in place and swayed back and forth on my mat as the ceremonial music played, enjoying every freedom these newfound truths offered me, but after a while, the nausea was just too much to bear. The Spirit in the plant gently instructed me to remove myself from the energy. I waved my hand and gestured for the assistance of one of the volunteers who came over to help me up and we proceeded to walk.

She asked me if I needed to go to the bathroom and while I hadn't thought of that before, it sounded like a good idea. I said yes, sounds good. I couldn't wait to get there, I felt so sick! I felt very weak in the knees and intoxicated, the world was spinning on its axis. As I approached the small outdoor Porta-Potty, the ego started to rise up. I *did not* want to use this "roughing it" style bathroom!

## The Masculine Spirit in the Plant

As I entered the small stall, the Spirit in the medicine shifted. No longer was I being coddled and nurtured by the feminine energy of Aya's Motherly love. I was now in the energy of the very authoritative, disciplinary, and masculine Spirit of Father God. I felt very much like a child being disciplined, but I was not afraid. As I sat on the toilet, the face of this big, bold, beautifully regal Black Panther appeared behind my closed eyes.

This masculine Spirit spoke to me in a roaring but comprehensible tone. He said, "Every snake that has ever entered into your body is about to come out." Just as crappy as the situations were when the penises entered my vagina, so too would their energy exit from my being as toxic waste! I could not get off the pot until I purged the spirits of every male that had ever entered my body, except, of course, my husband, Eric.

The solid and unbroken chain of snakes, which had been woven together by my past experiences, went straight down the toilet drain! I felt a deep sense of relief, unlike I had never known. It was as if every energetic link I had to any person who had ever molested or raped me and every male with whom I had a demonic soul tie was broken.

I had been detoxed. I felt innocent and pure all over again! I also felt a strong sense of confidence and presence within myself that I hadn't even known I'd lost. My surroundings no longer mattered. I sat on the toilet in pure bliss! I thanked God with deep sincerity and reverence for guiding my feet to this healing experience.

*"If God doesn't discipline you as he does all of his children, it means that you are illegitimate and are not really his children at all." ~Hebrews 12:8 NLT*

I thought the worst of my spanking was over. To my surprise, I was hit with another heavy bout of nausea. I tried to get up as I thought of how inappropriate it would be to throw up in the same tight quarters where I had just defecated, but the medicine would not let go of its grip!

The energy of the masculine Spirit roared as it pressed a very heavy, yet unseen field of energy against the lower half of my body, forcing me right back down on the toilet! I surrendered to the fact that I needed to take the whooping I was brought to receive in this lone Porta-Potty! Okay, okay ... I said, but can I at least flush the toilet? My request was granted.

While I was shuffling around to flush the toilet, the volunteer asked me if I wanted the bucket. She must have read my mind or felt my soul. I reached through the curtain of the Porta-Potty and gabbed for the bucket. Still resisting. The Spirit in the plant had enough and forced my purge by flashing before my closed eyes the image of the pastor's penis heading towards my mouth!

The vomit rushed up and out of me like a river without a dam! I welcomed it. Suddenly, I wanted to throw up every possible penis that had crossed my lips! I was feeling *light* and *fully free* from any demonic spirits that had entered me through my past sexual experiences.

I reached through the green curtain to hand my bucket back to the volunteer. When I stood up, preparing to exit the stall, Mother Aya returned and stopped me. SHe told me that I could not pull back the curtains and leave the stall until I remembered my name. I stood up tall, held my head up high, pulled my shoulders back, and spoke my name audibly. I felt a strong sense of dignity, gratitude, identity, confidence, and self-love.

As I pulled back the curtains, the Spirit in the plant gave me a simultaneous vision. In that vision, those curtains were not just the bathroom curtains with a pattern of the forest and little green frogs. They were the curtains I would walk through onto the stage of life. Before I ever step out onto any stage, before the curtains ever rise, I will know who I am. I will know my name.

I am Sabrina Universal Lawton. I am who I am, not through man's laws, but through the universal laws of love. I am a sun goddess. I was given a heavenly heart of turquoise aquamarine to share with you. I have been called to this life to embody the love of God, which is also in you. Yes, I have a *divine calling* in the earth. More importantly, *so do you.*

*"You made them a little lower than the angels;*
*you crowned them with glory and honor*
*and put everything under their feet."*
*~Hebrews 2:7-8 ESV*

As I washed my hands and rinsed my mouth with soap, the feminine Spirit in the plant instructed me to return to my mat underneath the large nurturing tree, so that SHe could tell me my whole life story. I began my walk, head held high, feeling sure-footed and ready for the gifts of love I was about to receive. I felt such peace and oneness with everyone and everything around me. When I returned and lay down on my mat, a miracle happened. Aya played the entire movie of my life through the motion picture screen of my mind behind my closed and eager eyes.

The ceremonial music and I were one. I caught every beat, every chord, every instrument. Every note and I were in unison. The Taita, who some might call our Shaman, felt my spirit. I could feel him join his spirit with mine as he stood there, towering over my head, playing the most beautiful melodies of love through his instrument.

In my inner vision, I saw myself dancing in heaven with Jesus, Maya Angelou, my Uncle Bruce, who was my true father figure, and a few others. We danced with pure joy and excitement! I could not see their faces, I could only feel their facial expressions. I could look down and see our happy feet, all dancing in a circle of love. We were having a party for me!

Jesus and I had a playful dance-off before he allowed me to win. We laughed and hugged before I was given a final and most beautiful vision of my husband and I in our old age. We were walking healthily, beautifully, and blissfully along a beach of white sand and turquoise waters situated just outside of our home.

The curtains to the screenplay of my life had finally closed. *Selah.* What an outstanding performance, God! There was nothing left to do but get on my hands and knees, place my face to the ground, and give God thanks and praise!

## Sadaf's Ayahuasca Journey

Years back, while vacationing in South Africa, I met a lovely young lady named Sadaf. She is originally from Tehran, Iran, but resided in the United States for most of her life. We were on the same tour bus and would be in close proximity over the next two weeks. Our fully packed itinerary included the enjoyment of places like Johannesburg, Soweto, Karongwe National Wildlife Reserve, and other landmarks and experiences along the way to the Cape of Good Hope in Cape Town.

The most memorable of my moments with Sadaf was when we rode together on the back of the most gentle, intelligent giant I had ever seen. There were probably five or six of us atop the high back of that beautifully regal elephant. Sadaf was right behind me and I've got the pictures to prove it!

She and I had a few good conversations about God during our trip as well. I had recently begun my work as a Spiritual Advisor and Sadaf was very interested in hearing more about my services. Shortly after we returned to the United States, Sadaf became a client. We worked together a number of times over the course of a few years and when our work was done, we remained good friends. Sadaf was inspired to continue her spiritual journey with the aid of plant medicines.

Ayahuasca came up a few times during our conversations. We talked of experiencing this sacred plant together, but as it turned out, I experienced the plant before she did. We spoke shortly after my return and she listened with full attention while I shared my experience. By the time our conversation ended, I knew Sadaf's Aya journey would be fast approaching. Sure enough, Sadaf called me about a month later to report that she too had recently returned from a plant medicine ceremony.

## Here's a powerful snippet of her story:

"Yes Ma'am," I said without any hesitation when she instructed me to *"take back the baby"* and hold him. Based on my experience with Mother Aya the night before, I knew better than to resist what was happening. The more I resisted her and the more I resisted my truths, the rougher my journey became. Aya reminded me often "You only get more of what you resist." We became acquainted very fast! I learned her ways quite quickly!

I grew up traveling the world with my family and was exposed to multiple religions and cultures. In my adult life, I would find myself swimming in a whirlpool of different beliefs and teachings. I always resonated with Jesus, but not quite the Bible, until I met my beautiful soul sister, Sabrina, who helped me read the Bible through a different lens. Admittedly, I would call on Jesus occasionally, but hadn't fully trusted or embodied his love as it was written.

Imagine my shock and initial resistance when Mother Mary appeared in my plant medicine journey and placed baby Jesus in my arms! Jesus was the baby I tried to give back to Mother Aya. "Raise him up," she said with the most bright and beautiful smile ... "Embody him." My hands were shaking a little, but as I started repeating my safe words *"Trust and Faith,"* a sense of lightness and calm overtook my body. I was able to hold baby Jesus without resistance.

As baby Jesus started fading away from my arms, God, Mother Aya, my Grandpa (who passed many years ago), and Jesus all gathered around me, radiating pure love! I fell in love with God, Jesus, and the Holy Spirit all over again, but this time, it felt very different. It didn't feel like a connection based on the words and instructions of others, but a *oneness* through what was a very beautiful, real, and life-changing experience.

## Precautions about the Plant Medicine

I do not claim that plant medicines are every person's pathway to God. I sincerely believe that if God calls you to the plant, the plant will find you. I answered the call of the Spirit to the plant kicking and screaming! I did not want to go. I am ever so grateful that I persisted in following not what people, religion, and fear told me, but what my intuition told me to do.

Do not partake in this sacred plant medicine without following the "Dieta," a specific set of preparatory guidelines provided by your ceremonial facility. I do not suggest you partake in plant medicines if you have not done some level of healing work to help prepare you emotionally for the truths they will reveal. The detox can be brutal, but the cleansing is blissful!

I am clear that God called me to Ayahuasca to *personally* provide me with the tools I needed to fulfill my destiny. When I heard HEr call, I fought through the fears and answered. It was the most awesome encounter with God I ever had.

Just as SHe said, "The Kingdom of Heaven is in your midst." I have answered my calling to share the truths about God and sex as they have been stored in the filing cabinets of my mind and the depths of my heart and soul. What truths are you called to speak? Who are you called to help set free?

Are these plant medicines good or bad for you? I've given you a few examples of what has followed the consumption of such plants, and there's much research you can do on your own accord. In the end, *you will know a tree by its fruit.*

> *"No good tree bears bad fruit, nor does a bad tree bear good fruit. For each tree is known by its own fruit."*
> *~Luke 6:43-44 NIV*

# Chapter 9: Evolve to Love

*"You can't fix a problem with the same consciousness or thinking that got you into the situation."*
*~Albert Einstein*

It is imperative that we understand the implications of a world currently under the temporary control of Satan. Evil spirits have created such persuading illusions that what may seem right is actually wrong, and what may seem wrong, might be just right! Here are a few examples of the beliefs we must collectively flip and reexamine in an effort to discover the truth by way of the fruit:

- Money will make you happy

- Plant medicines are not of God

- Religion is the only pathway to God

- Women cannot be direct messengers of God

- Children are not as intelligent or enlightened as adults

- Jesus is an attractive white man with long brown hair

- Melano people are less valuable than Caucasian people

The truth is that women have very powerful and noteworthy attributes of God, the obvious one being our ability to create man. Women also possess the instinctual ability to communicate with empathy and love and to nurture the young and fragile. Our monthly cycles, which are still widely misunderstood by both men and women, give us the ability to shed at the cellular level what no longer serves us, while sending a message to our bodies that this is a time to *be still and know.*

Women, if we allow our pre-menstrual cycles to serve us, we would receive more spiritual insight about the misalignments in our lives and our world. The more you use this time to sit in complete communion with God, the more you will understand your role in bringing about the solutions. Imagine the unprecedented progress we would make in our world by having a strong feminine presence as part of peace negotiations and conflict resolutions.

Money is clearly not the solution to our problems. Wealthy CEOs still commit suicide, and many a Hollywood star crashes and burns well before their time. I believe Michael Jackson was an outstanding performer. I also believe that he who died at the unsuspecting age of fifty by way of a prescription drug overdose, never truly found the spiritual reconciliation he needed to heal from the emotional pain caused by his lost childhood.

Imagine how mind-warping it would be to one's self-identity to be a little "black" boy, raised in a racist society where colored folks weren't allowed to drink out of the same water fountains, enter the same restaurants, or use the same bathrooms as "white" people. With all the racial tensions around him, he was given a temporary "free pass" because his spiritual gifts were desired for the mere entertainment of "white" audiences across America. We all took note of the damage done to his body. What kind of damage was created in his soul?

Marilyn Monroe was one of the most popular sex symbols and top-bill actresses in the 1950's. Her lifestyle afforded all types of luxury, fame, and fortune. It was all short-lived when she died of an overdose in her home at just thirty-six years of age. Let the untimely deaths of Prince, Whitney Houston and her daughter, Bobbi Kristina Brown, Anthony Bourdain, Kate Spade, and the many other stars who crash and burn be a wake-up call to the idea that money, world travel, fortune, or fame will solve your problems. *"Every problem has a spiritual solution."*

## Human Race Relations

Don't you find it fascinating that whenever you observe babies and children at play, there is absolutely no focus on race or skin color? They play joyfully for as long as they can, and it upsets them to be pulled apart. Unfortunately, when it comes to race relations, many have grown older, not wiser.

You have probably noticed that I do not generally use the terms "black" or "white" when referring to the race of Americans. First, we are the only culture that refers to ourselves and each other as a "color," and neither color is actually our true hue. Secondly, if we are going to address racism, we are going to have to stop with all the smoke-and-mirrors and call a thing a thing!

Darker-skinned people across the globe have been undermined and hidden in plain sight. When you walk the streets of Cuba, India, Brazil, and many other countries across the globe, the faces you see and the people you meet will likely have much more melanin than the faces advertised on the big screens representing such countries.

The root cause for racism is an issue with *melanin,* which is responsible for creating pigment in the skin and eyes, as well as providing other life-extending health benefits. For these reasons, I refer to melanin-dominant Americans as Melano and melanin-recessive Americans as Caucasian.

It does not sit well with me to continue the use of a word that has been programmed by man to carry the following vibrational energy frequency: b-lack. There has been a dark force of energy, disguised as light, trying to associate being black with a state of lacking. That same force is busy attempting to associate being white with things of great height like purity or being higher than everyone else. Just google search the definitions of both words and see for yourself.

Some of my *Melano* fellow people may want to refute this point by saying that we should continue using the terminology "black" because it's not about them; it's about us and what we do with the word. To you, I reply, we tried that already with the use of the N-word. How would you say that's working out? The fact is that this is not just a black and white issue. Racism affects many people with deeper degrees of melanin around the world and the time is now to address it globally.

Each year, scientists get together behind closed doors in an attempt to understand and replicate the many life-extending functions of melanin. My message to my fellow deeply pigmented Melano people around the world, "Let no one cause you to forget, you are beautifully, lovingly, and powerfully made!"

Here is a glimpse of the beauty and wonder of melanin as created by God:

"Melanin—and specifically, the form called eumelanin, is the primary pigment that gives humans the coloring of their skin, hair, and eyes. More importantly, it neutralizes free radicals in the body and the brain. Melanin protects the body from the hazards of ultraviolet and other radiation that can damage cells and lead to skin cancer, but why it is so effective at blocking such a broad spectrum of sunlight is still a mystery. Researchers at MIT and other institutions are opening the way for the development of synthetic materials that could have similar light-blocking properties."

Has the question ever crossed your mind about why it is common to see an image of Jesus being depicted as having white skin with long hair? Is this congruent with how he is described in the bible? When King Herod was seeking to kill him as a young child, Jesus's earth parents, Mary and Joseph, fled to Egypt which *is* in Africa. Common sense would tell you that you don't hide out where you stand out. The truth is, we are all made in the image and likeness of Jesus Christ.

> *"Therefore, if anyone is in Christ, he is a new creation. The old has passed away; behold, the new has come."*
> *~2 Corinthians 5:17 ESV*

Love loves all people, no matter how much or how little melanin you have. That does not negate the fact that if we are going to win the war between the flesh and the spirit, we must speak the truth about *everything.* No longer will white elephants in the room be tolerated. Issues of racism are indeed issues of the flesh—issues we absolutely *must* transcend.

The truth does hurt at times, but as the old adage goes, no pain— no gain. It is only when we travel through the often painful truth that we are set free. I am certain that with all the negative publicity "Melano" people have gotten historically, a few paragraphs of positivity are more than noteworthy.

If the desire of religion is to be truly effective, it would make addressing these serious matters a priority as an integral part of its healing modalities. Jesus was aware of how Satan would flip the script, turning religion against religion, men against women, the rich against the poor, and melanin-recessive against melanin-dominant people, which is why he said:

> *"But many who are first will be last, and many who are last will be first." ~Matthew 19:30 NIV*

When I was a young girl, I had a vivid dream that I have always remembered. There I sat, alone, in a cave that overlooked a beautiful and vast body of water. For quite a while, I sat—sad, alone, and melancholy. Just me and a gray, two-drawer filing cabinet. All of a sudden, I decided to get up and take flight over that vast, beautiful body of water.

My flight was peaceful, quiet, and serene. I flew right through the revolving glass doors of what seemed to be a library, or at least a place where there was a wealth of wisdom and knowledge. This book contains the contents that were kept in that gray, two-drawer filing cabinet, scheduled for delivery at such a time as this.

You *evolve to love* when you realize that love is not found in someone you seek; love is found in becoming who you are. The only way to be who you were created to be is to *know thyself.* Who are you? You are pure, unadulterated love. To help you remember, God has given you the *Universal Laws of Love* in plain sight. Make it a priority to seek embodiment.

## The Way of Love

*"If I speak in the tongues of men and of angels, but have not love, I am a noisy gong or a clanging cymbal. And if I have prophetic powers, and understand all mysteries and all knowledge, and if I have all faith, so as to remove mountains, but have not love, I am nothing. If I give away all I have, and if I deliver up my body to be burned, but have not love, I gain nothing. Love is patient and kind; love does not envy or boast; it is not arrogant or rude. It does not insist on its own way; it is not irritable or resentful; it does not rejoice at wrongdoing, but rejoices with the truth. Love bears all things, believes all things, hopes all things, endures all things."*
*~1 Corinthians 13:1-7 ESV*

It is God who animates you. You have been called to walk in the Spirit. You have direct access to The Holy Spirit, who is waiting patiently to assist you in learning to use your story for God's glory. You need not wait for physical death to experience

Heaven. You need not imagine hell; many people are living a hell of a life every day! God is here now. In all things. In all beings. God is in both the jaguar and the butterfly. God is in your fall and in your rise. God is in the yin and the yang. God is in you.

If you see yourself as just a body and not a soul, your life can be likened to the walking dead. The powerful, yet unseen, breath of God cannot flow freely through you. You will have new life when you realize that the *sole* purpose of your body is to use the *soles* of your feet to carry out your *soul's* mission. Do not allow vanity or the ego to keep you from doing what you came here to do. You are here to activate God in the earth through the power of your love.

*"For the entire law is fulfilled in keeping this one command: 'Love your neighbor as yourself.'" ~Galatians 5:14 NIV*

## Barriers to Love

If God is Love, and love is the solution, then why is loving ourselves so difficult to do? For decades, I did not love myself because growing up in a family in which there was an undercurrent of colorism made me feel like I wasn't as loved as my lighter-skinned, green-eyed younger brother.

This whole "whiter is righter" syndrome humanity is suffering from has created a vibration of self-hate that flows silently through many family trees. The backfire is that the light person secretly wishes to be darker and the dark person secretly wishes to be lighter—neither of them truly loves themselves.

I didn't love myself because, most of my life, I heard so much of what was wrong with me and so little about what was right. I didn't love myself because I hated the things I did, looking for love in all the wrong places. I didn't love myself because my religion and my culture caused me to walk through life with a verdict of *guilty* hanging over my head. I didn't love myself because I believed God didn't love me.

The ego I created and presented to the world to hide my low self-esteem shouted loudly and consistently, "See? I am beautiful! "Men fall for me left and right. See me ... Touch me ... Feel me ...." The ego always wanted to be fed but could never be filled.

I was exhausted trying to keep up with its demands by going to the gym or wearing makeup just to leave the house each day, or constantly being concerned about whether a man was looking at me. I knew that the only way for me to break free was to tell the truth: I didn't love myself. I didn't believe I was beautiful. I would soon discover I had no clue what true beauty really was. My barriers to love came crashing down when I asked God to show me who SHe is and who I am.

In my line of work as a Spiritual Advisor, I have discovered that although many are taught through religion that God is Love, most people tend to believe in a God who would treat them as their parents treated them. If you had loving parents, you were open to the idea that God is a loving God. If you had strict, authoritative parents who made you perform for their acceptance and approval, you might believe that God expects you to be perfect in order to receive HEr Love.

As they commonly say in the workplace, people don't leave their jobs because of their employer. They leave because they have issues with their direct supervisor. In the same way, we create a relationship with God which is often reflective of our experience with other humans, usually our parents or grandparents. Question whether or not this is working for you and ask God to show you who SHe really is.

*"The Lord is near to all who call on him, to all who call on him in truth." ~Psalm 145:18 ESV*

If you desire to have a closer relationship with God, reevaluating what you believe and why you believe it is an absolute necessity. Your family pathology plays an important role in how you see things. There are energy frequencies or patterns of behavior within the roots of your generational tree seeking to exist and thrive through you.

How can the fruit ever not be like the seed that produced it? The energies, spirits, or generational curses *(whichever terminology you choose)* will continue to travel from offspring to offspring, bearing the same fruit, unless and until someone recognizes the ungodly patterns of beliefs and behaviors and decides they no longer desire the often soul-shattering consequences. Ask God in prayer, with sincerity and in truth, to help you *see life through new lenses.*

The process of becoming new will require you to get your hands dirty as you dig up the roots, chop off the branches, and throw them into the fiery trials you will face in the transition! Like a farmer, these are the steps you must take before you can plant new seeds and bear a new harvest of *Love's Fruit* in the garden of your life.

## His-Story Repeats Itself

Look for repeated beliefs and patterns of behavior in your bloodline. What common behavioral traits do you see in your mother, your father, your grandmothers and grandfathers, your aunts, uncles, cousins, sisters, or brothers? What gifts did they give you? What chains must you break? *His-Story* repeats itself until it is healed.

You did not create the negative patterns of thoughts, beliefs, and behaviors that exist through you on your own; however, you *do* have a responsibility to identify and address patterns which do not serve you. Just know, you cannot use the same thinking that caused you to repeat the patterns to change them. In other words, the computer with the virus doesn't know it is sick. But there is good news. All you need to do is ask for help and God will bring to your aid the people, plants, perspective, or whatever it is you need to help you write a new life story. Monitor your mind and value your thoughts. Think only on things which bring light into your life, for it is both your thoughts and the words which follow that created the life you have today.

If you could read the words on the walls of your home, your bed, your bathroom mirror, your car, your office, your mind ... what would they say? Allow your awareness of these emotional energies to inform you of where you are, then shift your focus in the direction of God's Will.

*"Words are things. You must be careful, careful about calling people out of their names, using racial pejoratives and sexual pejoratives and all that ignorance. Don't do that. Someday we'll be able to measure the power of words. I think they are things. They get on the walls. They get in your wallpaper. They get in your rugs, in your upholstery, and your clothes, and finally in to you." ~Maya Angelou*

## Forget to Remember

*"No, dear brothers and sisters, I have not achieved it, but I focus on this one thing: Forgetting the past and looking forward to what lies ahead, I press on to reach the end of the race and receive the heavenly prize for which God, through Christ Jesus, is calling us." ~Philippians 3:13-14 NLT*

When you transcend the pain of your past and *evolve to love*, you will meet the most joyful, abundant, beautiful, authentic version of you. To remember who you are, begin the work of "forgetting" who the world taught you to be. You must go against the grain and undergo the arduous process of excavating the feelings and stagnant energy that have accumulated within you from your past experiences.

The memories of pain and disappointment and the secrets hidden behind your mind's eye must be brought to the light. You *Keep Your Sexy Sacred* when you remove unhealthy energetic vibrations from your *inner being* by speaking your truths out into the atmosphere.

Darkness cannot live when exposed to the light. Darkness thrives in the hidden places, the cracks and crevasses untouched by the Light of the Son. For this reason, you are only as sick as your secrets. Speak your truth so that God can send to your aid just what you need to help you forget who the world taught you to be and remember who you are. You are light, you are love, you are forgiven, you are a god—just a little lower than the angels. We are *all together* the One Body.

*"Now you are the body of Christ and individually members of it." ~1 Corinthians 12:27 ESV*

Rejoining the Body is a divine dance between remembering and forgetting. Let me forewarn you: this work of *undoing* and *integration* will require the painful process of extracting layer upon layer of what can be summed up as ego. As with anything in life, for something new to be born, some form of death to the life it once knew must occur.

A pregnant woman must die to being pregnant in order for her unborn child to experience life on earth. A seed in the ground must crack open and die in order to produce the beautiful fragrance of its flower or fruit. So, too, must you die to your old self to become new, just as with the metamorphosis of a caterpillar to a butterfly. This tight and uncomfortable, yet liberating, process will leave you with a blank canvas or "light space" you'll need to transform and co-create your life with God.

## Ask yourself: What must die within me to become new?

I had to die to the idea that my external beauty was for men. Instead of being hypercritical of myself, I learned to see my beauty and my flaws as glorious reflections of the temple of God, divinely designed to carry out HEr message: *Keep Your Sexy Sacred*. Wouldn't it be like God to use a woman who might be considered *sexy* to tell the world that vanity and preoccupation with the flesh are killing us? I am eternally grateful for the purpose my temple serves; I take no pride in the temple itself.

This is where the billion-dollar fashion and makeup industry has caused women to go astray. Women have been deceived into believing that our body temples should be perfectly painted and adorned on the outside as displays of value. While I encourage dressing up to look and feel beautiful, so much time is spent on creating curb appeal that when one enters the temple, they find it empty and void of all treasures. Those who enter steal the remnants of any value which remained, leaving the temple even more desolate than before. This woman soon becomes an empty, nicely decorated shell, and the return on the investment in her beauty products is void.

*"Do you not know that you are God's temple and that God's Spirit dwells in you?" ~1Corinthians 3:16 ESV*

## Change Your Mind

The mind is, in its simplest description, a video recorder which good, bad, lovely, or ugly wants to replay itself over and over and over again. In the most undetectable ways, it is on a constant quest to return to its baseline modality. The mind will seek to retell its story to anyone who will hear it, as many times as is necessary in an effort to keep its learned identity alive. The mind, as it was formed by your experiences, seeks to survive as it was created, and often at the expense of its host—you.

Your mind remembers the prominent *emotions* you felt early on in life. You have identified these emotions as *you*. Did you ask for the experiences that caused these *energies in motion* to be transferred into you? My guess is likely not. These feelings are not you, but they have taken up residence within you. Without you, where would they go? The moment you recognize what these energies are and what they thrive on, you can serve an eviction notice! You are not your mind. Your mind is yours. Change your thoughts, change your mind, and *evolve to love*.

*"Preach the word; be ready in season and out of season; reprove, rebuke, and exhort, with complete patience and teaching." ~2 Timothy 4:2 ESV*

You've heard the saying: Birds of a feather flock together. It is no coincidence that positive people find other positive people to hang around and negative people find other negative people to fraternize with. Scholars tend to connect with other scholars, violent men know other violent men, men of the cloth converse with other men of the cloth ... and so on and so forth.

We are all connected by an unseen and unbroken force of energy or spirit. Like radio stations, there are many frequencies that exist in the airwaves all at once, and we are all tuned in to one station or another. Just as the winds in the north are somehow connected by an inseparable thread to the winds of the south, east, and west, so too are we all connected to one another. For this reason, what you put out into the universe *vibrationally* will surely come back to you in people, places, and things.

In the Eastern world, this may be referred to as *karma*. Karma is indeed a universal law, which if described in the Western world would sound a little more like: *you reap what you sow*. Thankfully, there is another universal law called *grace*. When called upon, grace will restore your dignity, crown you with honor, show you mercy, and make your mess your message.

*"Turn your wounds into wisdom."* ~Oprah Winfrey

## Understanding the Ego

The ego is in direct opposition to God and is therefore in direct opposition to you. Many have referred to the ego as *Edging God Out*. Another way to describe the ego is as the personality you created in an effort to protect yourself from emotional pain. In most cases, this pain began somewhere in your past, and, for many, it began in childhood.

As long as the ego is present, you can be sure that there is a wounded child within, seeking to resolve past transgressions. The irony is that the persona you created to protect you will likely reconnect you with the same feelings and emotions you're trying so hard to avoid. Only now, the pain is self-inflicted.

The ego is all about the little "i." The problem is, there is no "i" in love. We live in a vast universe! Each of us has the unique fingerprint of God, yet we spend exhaustive amounts of emotional energy trying to portray an image of our lives based on what we want other people to see.

Too many of us care too much about what other people think, so we wear masks and create illusions to the point that we quickly forget who we are. Just think about the one trillion selfies and perfect portrayals of far too many lives on social media. If you are ever tempted to get caught up in what you *think* someone else's life looks like, remember how they make you feel. *Energy doesn't lie.*

Technology is a great gift to humanity. It is responsible for the mass distribution of awakening information we have access to online today. The issue is not the technology. The issue is the disrespect and lack of understanding we have with regard to its uses.

Our children are sitting right next to one another, texting instead of talking, and many people are so busy creating "fake-books" that they have lost sight of their true identity. Let's not forget about the exorbitant amount of time being wasted on simply "browsing." What about the people who need you when you lay down your devices? How much time and energy are you giving to the one who needs you the most—you?

*"And what do you benefit if you gain the whole world but lose your own soul?" ~Mark 8:36 NLT*

We all vacillate in varying degrees between the ego and the soul of who we are. How often you experience life through the lens of one or the other is highly dependent upon your Spiritual IQ®. For this reason, connecting with God and walking in the spirit of love is a daily practice.

None of us, as long are we are in this flesh realm, will ever wake up and say, I need not meditate, pray, or connect with God today. You will regularly be presented with opportunities to transcend the ego and walk in the spirit. This is a necessary process for building up the spiritual muscle you'll need to answer God's calling on your life.

## Transcending the Ego

The energetic vibration associated with the ego does not always feel like the bad guy. In fact, it seems to be your best friend. It comes to your aid each time you call upon it. You can always rely on it when you feel your heart needs protection and, of course, when you feel the need to be right! For these reasons, you may feel more inclined to let it stick around. The issue is, because the ego was born of and receives its life force from the pain that created its existence, it has no choice but to create that same kind of pain in order to survive.

While preparing to deliver the messages packaged within these passages, I have had to power through what the ego has been telling me in an effort to try and *protect me*: *What about your relatives? What are people going to think? What if they misunderstand? What are they going to say about you? What about this, and what about that? You should play it safe. You sure you want to do this?* All to keep me from doing the very thing that God has created me to do. God is the *Still Small Voice*. To the loud, constantly nagging voice screaming in my head, I respond: "Peace. Be still. This book is my release of any power you have over me. Sealed with a *KYSS*."

## Ego Identity

A young woman I worked with moved frequently as a child from state to state and school to school. This caused her to feel isolated and alone, like she didn't belong. Now, an adult, whenever she enters a room filled with people she doesn't know, she covers her feelings of discomfort and not belonging with her style, poise, and a very well-put-together appearance. Initially, she doesn't make much eye contact and stays to herself.

How do you feel in a room with such a person? Do you get a warm and inviting feeling, or do you get a twinge of discomfort and feel more inclined to shy away? The ego that this young woman created to protect herself was actually keeping her trapped in the same exact emotional energy as in her childhood.

Thankfully, she was able to write a new story when she had the courage to walk back through the defining moments from her past and look again with 20/20 vision, through the lenses of love. Love will always give grace and create space between the words "imperfect" and "I'm perfect." No matter what has happened to you or through you, you are perfect just as you are. It is all a matter of how you see it. Connecting with your own internal truth will set you free.

I once held the subconscious belief that physical beauty was the only real gift I had to offer. The seeds of vanity and lust were watered by that belief. And trying to be beautiful all the time didn't make me feel very beautiful at all. These repetitive thoughts on the flesh ultimately gave way to my misdeeds. I ate of the fruit of sexual immorality, which tasted sweet going down but would inevitably make me sick to my stomach!

*"As the Scriptures say, 'People are like grass; their beauty is like a flower in the field. The grass withers and the flower fades.'"*
*~1 Peter 1:24 NLT*

The root cause of my suffering was that my ego was in direct opposition to my spirit. God is aware of the painful paradoxes our worldly experiences have created within us. God is eagerly waiting for you to *ask* for your spiritual solutions. Surrender the ego and the things the ego has caused you to do. Remember whose you are and allow Love to love you back to life.

## Your Belief Will Be Life

When Moses asked God at the burning bush, *Who are you?* God said, "I Am, that I Am." Because you are made in the image and likeness of God, this same statement applies to you. Whatever you believe you are worthy of having, you will have. Whatever you believe you are, you will be.

This universal, yet simple, law suggests that you will only ever hold in your reality what you have first held in your mind. Each day, take a few moments to imagine yourself doing the things you love to do, being in the places you love to be, and sharing your life with those you love.

Speak life into your life. Life and death are in the power of the tongue because words are living things. Words mark the first steps towards the actions that follow your predominant thoughts. Do not think of your dreams as distant dreams. *Feel into them now.* Believe that you already are who and where you desire to be.

Where are you? What are you doing? Who do you envision around you? Do you feel deep joy, gratitude, and love? You are at every given moment creating not what you want, but what you believe. Consciously or unconsciously, you are activating the following *divinity code*:

*Your <u>belief</u> will <u>be-life</u> for you.*

Believe big! The ego has no interest in your knowing that your mind cannot discern the difference between whether you are actually having these blissful experiences or simply dreaming them. The personal video recorder in your head will project into your reality whatever movie you play the most on the motion picture screen of your mind.

*"Do not be conformed to this world, but be transformed by the renewal of your mind, that by testing you may discern what is the will of God, what is good and acceptable and perfect."*
*~Romans 12:2 ESV*

# Chapter 10: Reevaluating Relationships

*Do not be deceived: "Bad company ruins good morals."*
*~1 Corinthians 15:33 ESV*

Now that you see clearly this whole new world that exists simultaneously within the world you once knew, what do you do? It will likely be the case that as you identify with who you are in the Spirit, your relationships with those closest to you will change.

Some of your greatest adversities may come from your closest family members and friends. It will make them uncomfortable to experience a version of you that does not fit within the confines of the box they put you in. Jesus has prepared you for such a time as this.

*"Then Jesus' mother and brothers came to see him, but they couldn't get to him because of the crowd. Someone told Jesus, 'Your mother and your brothers are outside, and they want to see you.' Jesus replied, 'My mother and my brothers are all those who hear God's word and obey it.'"~Luke 8:19-21 NLT*

Let not even your own mother, brother, sister, or children interfere with your walk of faith. Ask God to help you discern how to lovingly *protect your energy.* When I decided to walk in the spirit, the greatest adversities I experienced were with my mother.

While she did her best to support the new me, it seemed very difficult for her to believe that I could stop looking for love in all the wrong places, be it another affair, partying, smoking, drinking, or anything else that was reflective of the kind of false love I once sought. This is the woman who raised me. She knew my behavioral patterns very well. They were much like her own.

How dare you break free from the tradition of these repeated patterns of behavior running through our family tree? Who do you think you are to disrupt the spirits that have been travelling through our bloodline for generations? For some people, your light will begin to shine so brightly that it exposes things about themselves that they'd rather keep hidden in the darkness. Do not make their discomfort your concern. The only chance they ever have at *seeing* can only come by way of looking upon the light.

When it comes to the changes you want to see in your world, the first soul you must save is your own. Secure your own oxygen mask before attempting to give life to someone else. After you have helped yourself, God will send others to you who are *asking* to be free. Do not waste your breath trying to get anyone to change. That would be incongruent with the universal law in which one must ask and believe in order to receive.

*"Therefore I tell you, whatever you ask in prayer, believe that you have received it, and it will be yours." ~Mark 11:24 ESV*

The wisest people in the world don't go around spewing their thoughts and beliefs with rapid fire at just anyone. They know better than to waste their precious words on deaf ears. They have a gentle, quiet spirit, speaking only at their divinely appointed time and responding only to those who *ask*. They know better than to throw their pearls to swine.

*"Don't waste what is holy on people who are unholy. Don't throw your pearls to pigs! They will trample the pearls, then turn and attack you." ~Matthew 7:6 NLT*

Whenever you try to help someone who isn't asking, the person will likely take your offer, but not truly *receive* the gift because they did not ask or believe. You will end up emotionally drained and energetically depleted. I say again: *"protect your energy."*

I discovered that the more I evolved, the more aggressive the people around me became in their unconscious attempts to drain my sacred creative energy or life force. This happened like clockwork! Whenever I was in a state of peak personal performance, people would seemingly come from out of nowhere, seeking my attention. Do not be distracted.

Have you ever been on the cusp of your greatness? You decided you were going to move forward and do this or that. You were in it, believing and pressing through your doubts, fears, and the unknowns. Then someone called you out of the blue with news that threatened to knock you completely off the path. Do not at any cost allow those from your past to persist in redepositing the negative energy you are working so hard to purge.

If you feel inclined to provide a reason for your distance, tell them it's not about them, it's about you. You are seeking answers to questions and what you need most right now is stillness with God. If self-love prompts you, and you can do it with a heart of true forgiveness, it's okay to walk away.

*Love is a Shape-Shifter®*
*Love is whatever it needs to be whenever it needs to be it*
*Love is the relationship you lost that you never really needed*
*Love is the one you draw near to on every occasion*
*Love is the one you walk away from as an act of self-love and preservation*

173

*Love is the experience that woke you up from your past behavior*
*Love covers all transgressions, giving you grace and favor*
*Love is the pain which caused you to say, I've had enough!*
*Love calms your worry when the winds blow wildly and the seas*
*are rough ~Sabrina Universal Lawton*

## Severing Sexual Soul-ties

*"For we do not wrestle against flesh and blood, but against the rulers, against the authorities, against the cosmic powers over this present darkness, against the spiritual forces of evil in the heavenly places." ~Ephesians 6:12 ESV*

Have you been in a sexual relationship with a person who gives you all their "love and affection" whenever you're together; yet, when you're out of sight, you're out of mind? This is a sexual soul-tie. This type of relationship will bear the fruit of lust, lies, and loss, because this is the nature of the seeds sown. I have been there. It seemed as though whenever Micah and I (the neighbor I had the long-term affair with) were in close proximity, the energy of sex and sensuality was thick in the air.

His excitement would grow in my presence. And the smell of his cologne, the touch of his hair, and the way he felt was undoubtedly consuming to my senses. The fact that he showered me with compliments about how beautiful I was and looked into my eyes like he would eat me alive caused me to feel a rush of excitement that was frankly not my life. Lust is intoxicating. It causes you to enter a sort of drunken trance with or without alcohol.

Whenever I left Micah's presence, he would have me wondering how he could have come on so strong with his compliments, attention, and sexual energy and not even call or text me to see how my day was going. If you know this feeling, you know it feels like someone holding you close, then pulling you away and punching you in the stomach, over and over again. Yet, you keep going back, hoping for a different outcome. This is a *demonic soul-tie.* The root of it is deception.

*"...He was a murderer from the beginning. He has always hated the truth, because there is no truth in him. When he lies, it is consistent with his character; for he is a liar and the father of lies." ~John 8:44 ESV*

Satan is known as The Father of Lies. If there is deception in any relationship, you can be sure the vibrational energy of evil is in your midst. Don't forget that everything is energy and that we are all spirit. The spirits of your ancestors are to varying degrees *all* present within you and are a part of your genetic makeup. The spirit of the things you allow to enter into your body through your eyes are also present. The same holds true for the person you are sleeping with.

Are you allowing the spirit of light or the spirit of darkness to enter you? This is why you just can't stay away. You get twisted up with a person like this because through the soul-tie you created while having sex, you infuse your essence with theirs. They then become a part of your identity. The spirits of lust, lies, and deception have now grown in strength through your vessel, and they will do whatever it takes to continue using you as host.

The unsettling truth of this reality never hit me so hard as when during one of our last lustful rendezvous, Micah was having sex with me from behind. The room was kind of dark, but was lit by the light of the T.V. During our sexual interchange, I glanced over my shoulder behind me. What I saw scared me.

Micah had his arms stretched out wide in the air, on either side. His eyes were closed as he thrusted back and forth, his body moving in almost ritualistic waves. I could not believe what my eyes were showing me! Micah looked like a big, monstrous demon consuming every ounce of light I had from my *being*. Not only was I allowing Satan to suck the light out of me; I was simultaneously allowing seeds of darkness to be sown into my sacred space. Well, what do you know? All this time I was seducing men, Satan was seducing me.

## Spirits are Transferable

When spirits intermingle through sex acts, you are combining the most sacred parts of yourself with a mass field of energy that grows in power and intensity with every encounter. Spirits are transferred not just through the things we touch, but also the things we see. What spirits are being transferred through the viewing of pornography and violence?

Evil has an insatiable appetite. The spirit of lust and lies seeks and finds its next host until the result is death. The death of a relationship, the death of sound health, the death of a sound mind, and, its ultimate goal, the death of your ability to fulfill God's plan for your life.

*"The thief comes only to steal and kill and destroy. I came that they may have life and have it abundantly." ~John 10:10 ESV*

You are a player in this Great Game of Chess. Will you play the role of pawn, god, or goddess? Forgive yourself for not knowing what you did not know and forgive others for being unsuspecting players in the game. God is not concerned with what you did last summer or last night. God is excited about your return.

*"In the same way, there is more joy in heaven over one lost sinner who repents and returns to God than over ninety-nine others who are righteous and haven't strayed away!" ~Luke 15:7 NLT*

## The Imperative of Forgiveness

*"And Jesus said, 'Father, forgive them, for they know not what they do.'"~Luke 23:34 ESV*

Realize that people who are hurting tend to hurt other people because pain is the sum of all they have to give. No, they did not have a right to violate your heart and your trust nor did the ones who hurt them have a right to do so. You may be thinking, "I know this logically; however, it doesn't make the pain go away." You're right; it doesn't. The good news is that *there's power in your pain.*

Accessing this power requires you to understand this spiritual truth: you are not just a body. Whatever has been done to you in the physical realm has no power over your spirit. In fact, if you let it happen, God wants to use these transgressions for your good. Allow God to repurpose your pain.

When you stop focusing on the darkness of your past and remember the light which you are, you will see your painful experiences through the lenses of love. You will recognize that these experiences taught you the love lessons of compassion, understanding, wisdom, humility, and a number of other virtues that now support you in laying the desires of your flesh to rest and walking in the spirit.

It is no coincidence that those who decide not to become victims of their past often choose careers that allow them to help others overcome the very obstacles they have won victory over. In becoming the light that shines away the darkness, they forget the crushing blow of it all and focus on the gifts it gave them in terms of their ability to help others through like experiences. With this wisdom and understanding, all that remains is forgiveness and love.

Forgiveness takes practice. Saying to someone "I forgive you" doesn't negate the fact that you may be tempted to remember and reconnect with the pain they caused you to feel in the past. Hindsight is 20/20! Shift your emotional energy by reflecting on what you might have learned from the experience. You know you have forgiven someone when you can say, "Thank you *for-giving* me that experience" because you can see how God used it for your good.

Whenever you have a hard time forgiving, return to the peace of the present moment by engaging the following exercise using the acronym STOP as coined by Spiritual Advisor Deepak Chopra:

- **S**TOP
- **T**ake a Deep Breath
- **O**bserve your current situation
- **P**roceed in the present moment *with love*

Ask yourself, "Regardless of what I am thinking about a person or situation, is anyone actually hurting me in this moment—now? Am I free to *be* as I choose right now?" It was Deepak who also said, "The past is history, the future is a mystery, all we have is now."

The present moment is a powerful gift from God that allows you to fully engage with what your spirit exists to accomplish. Focus on the *now* to get an accurate understanding of yourself and your current situation. Come to the present moment to activate a liberating *divinity code* found in the power of now:

*When you are in the <u>now</u>*
*You have <u>won</u>*
*Because you <u>own</u> it*

## There's Power in Your Pain

I am grateful to have discovered the power in my pain. I am grateful for every hardship, every mistake, and every heartbreak. I am thankful to my mom for doing the best she could with what she had. The matters of the heart she had to deal with kept her from being more present with me. While I would have loved her presence, her distance gave me thick skin and taught me how to fend for myself at an early age.

Thank you, mom, for the tumultuous walk you walked in this life. I hear your tears as a thousand raindrops. I know you loved me just as much as you could love yourself. I am thankful that you were cast a starring role on the motion picture movie screen of my life. I pray that love, peace, and the fullness of joy be your rewards in heaven.

I have always loved my handwriting. My biological father would occasionally send me letters from prison over the years. I quickly noticed how our handwriting and writing styles were strikingly similar! I thank my dad for giving me the gift of his amazing penmanship and writing style.

I thank my dad also for the time he had phone sex with me. This was the code that helped create the virus: *inappropriate relationship with man = love.* Without having this program downloaded into my being, I would have never had the opportunity to seek God's face and help God's children *win the war between the flesh and the spirit.*

I thank God for every disappointment, and every divine delay. Without them, I would have never known the power of prayer. I thank God for allowing the molestation, rape, abuse, introduction to porn, and sexually immoral behavior in which I engaged. I thank God for every mistake I made which killed me ever so softly, until all that was left for me to do was turn my face toward the *Son*.

Without this walk through the valleys and the shadows of death, I would not have sought after, nor acquired, the *divinity codes* necessary to guide you along the narrow road to life—and life more abundantly.

*"But small is the gate and narrow the road that leads to life, and only a few find it" ~Matthew 7:14. NIV*

## Your Story, God's Glory

There was a little girl who grew up feeling different from as far back as she could remember. She didn't look upon her outward beauty and those around her really didn't either. All she wanted was love, yet experienced pain since she was born. This broke her heart into a million pieces, and she became a woman scorned. Still, she pressed through life with her dreams in her soul and her gifts in her spirit. Considering what she had endured, she did much better than most perceived of her. Although she put her best foot forward, those closest to her didn't really believe in her.

As she began to grow and change, her family distanced themselves, while others silently judged her. Some greeted her with niceties, yet they never truly loved her. How could they? They truly knew nothing of her. She knew her success in life could only come by way of healing. No matter what anyone saw on the outside, she knew deep down she was divinity. She ran the race marked out for her with courage and perseverance. No one could take away her crown. She had the victory because she knew God's Love was all she truly needed.

If you heard your story in her-story, I am glad to have your good company! Look again. Not only is this our story, but this is also the story of Jesus Christ. Every step of the way, Jesus has empathized deeply with your walk in the flesh. He knew the darkness of this world would try to destroy you, but do not fear death. When you die to the lures of the flesh, you will rise to the life of the Spirit.

It makes sense why those closest to Jesus at his crucifixion were women: his mother, Mary, and his mother's sister, Mary, the wife of Clopas, and Mary Magdalene were right by his side. When Jesus was resurrected, he revealed himself first to the woman, Mary Magdalene. She was a devout disciple of Jesus who had seven demons casted out of her. Probably as many as were cast out of me! Jesus wants you to know that no matter how much the world has rejected you, your feminine God-power is what is needed to unleash heaven on earth.

*"Your kingdom come, your will be done, on earth as it is in heaven." ~Matthew 6:10 ESV*

To the men of the cloth who have blasphemed his name and made a caricature of his image, I interrupt your regularly scheduled programming to send you this public service announcement: With regard to Jesus, either speak his truth or "keep his name out yo' mouth!"

*"Many will say to Me on that day, 'Lord, Lord, did we not prophesy in Your name, and in Your name drive out demons and perform many miracles?' Then I will tell them plainly, 'I never knew you; depart from Me, you workers of lawlessness.'"*
*~Matthew 7:22-23 NIV*

181

# Chapter 11: We Get There To-Get-Her

*"Being asked by the Pharisees when the kingdom of God would come, he answered them, 'The kingdom of God is not coming in ways that can be observed, nor will they say, 'Look, here it is!' or 'There!' for behold, the kingdom of God is in the midst of you.'"* ~Luke 17:20-21 ESV

To experience the kingdom of God, you must press beyond your limiting beliefs. Our world is filled with scholars, theologians, and many scientists who have still not concluded the "big bang theory" improbable. The question they fail to ask is this: **"Why does life, by very virtue of design, function most optimally when nurtured by the power of love?"** Fear, hate, and other lower energy frequencies cause the breakdown and destruction of life and speed up the process of death and dis-ease. Who *"thought"* to create life in this way?

A profound study of water (which accounts for roughly 70 percent of our Earth's surface) helps illustrate the power our emotional energy has to create either beauty or destruction. In the late Dr. Masaru Emoto's *New York Times* Best Selling book, *The Hidden Secrets of Water*, Dr. Emoto proves by scientific experiments that water from clear springs and water that has been exposed to loving words shows brilliant, complex, and colorful snowflake patterns. In contrast, polluted water, or water exposed to negative words, forms incomplete, asymmetrical patterns with dull colors.

Like earth, your body is comprised of 70 percent water. What is the condition of the water-based blood flowing through your body? The implications of this research provide us with profound insight into the power our thoughts and words alone have in positively impacting our lives, our health, and our world.

*"In the beginning was the Word, and the Word was with God, and the Word was God." ~John 1:1 ESV*

To those who have been using the power of words to create with arrogance and pride, you have been running a virus as written in the following *divinity code:*

*Arrogance + Intellect = Artificial Intelligence.*

The error of A.I. is that it uses the gifts of ancient knowledge and technology without respect, discipline, or regard for God's intent. The evolution of humanity has very little to do with our EQ (Emotional Quotient) or our IQ (Intelligence Quotient). It has everything to do with our SQ (Spiritual Quotient).

*"For it is written: 'I will destroy the wisdom of the wise; the intelligence of the intelligent I will frustrate.' Where is the wise person? Where is the teacher of the law? Where is the philosopher of this age? Has not God made foolish the wisdom of the world?" ~1 Corinthians 1:19-20*

Not degrees, nor doctorates, nor doctrines, but *love* is the key that unlocks the doors of wisdom and understanding within the gates of heaven. The measure in which love is needed for us to collectively experience heaven on earth can only be acquired *together*. Look there, in the word together, and find another *divinity code:* we get there *to-get-**her**—the feminine nature of God.* Yes, these words are trustworthy and true. The only way to experience earth as it is in Heaven is to allow God's feminine energy to flow freely through you. Perhaps that's where that old adage comes from: "Happy wife. Happy life."

## A Father's Wise Instruction to His Son

*"Blessed is the one who finds wisdom,*
*and the one who gets understanding,*
*for the gain from her is better than gain from silver*
*and her profit better than gold.*
*She is more precious than jewels,*
*and nothing you desire can compare with her.*
*Long life is in her right hand;*
*in her left hand are riches and honor.*
*Her ways are ways of pleasantness,*
*and all her paths are peace.*
*She is a tree of life to those who lay hold of her;*
*those who hold her fast are called blessed.*
*The Lord by wisdom founded the earth;*
*by understanding he established the heavens;*
*by his knowledge the deeps broke open,*
*and the clouds drop down the dew.*
*My son, do not lose sight of these—*
*keep sound wisdom and discretion,*
*and they will be life for your soul*
*and adornment for your neck."*
*~Proverbs 3:13-22 ESV*

## Get Wisdom and Understanding

Wisdom and understanding are described in the feminine "she" and "her" energy frequencies repeatedly in the Bible. The book of *"PR-over-BS"* also points out that *she* has been with God since the beginning of time and that *she* is a *tree of life.* How can you tap into her wisdom and her understanding if you do not connect with *her* within yourself? Male and female. All beings have a natural balance of feminine and masculine energy in varying quantities according to their kind.

It is critical that you allow yourself to be fully you. Speak your heart, cry about it, give attention to the little child inside you who is sad, afraid, alone, and confused. Do not hold back your truth. Shine a light on your emotions and be set free.

Do you have a same-sex oriented family member? I have gay family members whom I love very much. I can only imagine how hard it must be at times for them to face the judgment and ridicule of others. Before you rush to judgment, remember: God does not think like man.

Perhaps because the universe is self-correcting, many of our same-sex-oriented populations are reflections of the Feminine and Masculine energy of the universe attempting to bring itself back to balance. If you persist in believing that being gay is a virus, love is the only cure.

*"Owe no one anything, except to love each other, for the one who loves another has fulfilled the law." ~Romans 13:8 ESV*

Just as there is a deviant side to heterosexuality, there is a deviant side to homosexuality. If you would like to begin your research on the root cause for deviant homosexual acts, the Roman Catholic Church gives you plenty documentation for a case study. The Catholic Church is at the top of the list of the largest

Christian church organizations in the world with approximately 1.3 billion baptized Catholics worldwide as of 2016.

As one of the oldest religious institutions, it has played a prominent role in the history and development of Western civilization. Gather the facts about the woeful impact these men of "god" have had on the young, innocent, and unsuspecting souls they have violated through rape, abuse, and hetero- and primarily homosexual abuse.

The massive virus running through the walls, halls, pews, pulpits, and men of the Catholic Church, quantifiably since the 1950's, is nothing more than the culmination of evil spirits who once lived backwards in those same fields of energy. The seeds of their doctrine which suggests only men can by *supernatural law* give spiritual life through priesthood and women can only by way of *natural law* give natural life by childbirth have taken root.

The fruit manifested is that women cannot represent God on the pulpit. Another more insidious manifestation is the apparent disdain for women, as shown by the overwhelming preference for boys and men. Analyze the fruit and do not be deceived.

## A Love Offering to God's Children

### Spiritual Brother,

I apologize for the wars you might have fought. I pray that God would remove the imagery and stench of senseless death from your soul. I apologize on behalf of anyone who ever told you things like *don't cry, toughen up, or stop acting like a pussy* whenever you expressed your more feminine qualities of God.

You were programmed very early on to believe that women are the weaker vessel, not just physically, but spiritually. Women have a purpose in this world which reaches far beyond your pleasure. Among many other things, women are designed to help you deepen your relationship with God. Test the theory. If you take honest inventory, you'll find that the quality of your relationship with women is a direct reflection of the quality of your relationship with God.

I apologize for any sexual violations you may have experienced at the hands of those who were under the spell of demonic spirits, whether you were violated by your grandparent, pastor, parent, cousin, uncle, aunt, stranger, or friend. These are all people you should have been able to trust. Forgive them. Leave their fate to God, and press forward with perseverance. You have been cleansed by the *living water* of God's word.

*"But whoever drinks of the water that I will give him will never be thirsty again. The water that I will give him will become in him a spring of water welling up to eternal life."*
*~John 4:14 ESV*

The devil lied when he told you that being loving, gentle, vulnerable, and emotionally connected with your *light* or *soft* feminine energies is a "gay" thing to do. He lied when he told you to feed your masculine energy until your appetite could not be quenched. Just as with all things of nature, God's creations are created in perfect harmony and balance. Hidden within the *balance* of your masculine and feminine energy are gifts from God. Be meek. Be respectful. Be loving. Be free. The Kingdom of Heaven has made you whole.

## Spiritual Sister,

I apologize on behalf of anyone who has ever pierced your heart, corrupted your mind, pillaged your body, and plundered your soul. No one should ever be subject to these acts of sexual deviancy, physical abuse, emotional pain, or any other trauma you might have endured.

Whether you were violated by your grandparent, pastor, parent, cousin, uncle, aunt, stranger, or friend, these are all people you should have been able to trust. Forgive them. Leave their fate to God. Press forward with perseverance. You have been cleansed by the *living water* of God's word.

*"Whoever believes in me, as Scripture has said, rivers of living water will flow from within them." ~John 7:38*

Rise up and stand in your power using the gifts of your feminine energy and often-suppressed masculine energy. Awaken the Jaguar in you! Let your yes be yes and your no be no. Say no to the men who keep robbing you from yourself and say yes to your God-given divinity. You will naturally draw spiritually-aligned men and women into your life.

I apologize that you've heard men say to other men, "Don't be a pussy." This may have subconsciously programmed you to believe your vagina is weak and that strength comes only with "balls" or "big cojones." Allow me to clear this up for you. Your sexy, sacred vagina is a powerful and glorious creation! It endures the pain of birthing new life and bounces right back to its glorious inner workings like clockwork.

The masculine scrotum or *"balls"* are extremely fragile and cannot tolerate even the tap of the knee. Certainly, men have a special package to deliver us. They carry the seeds we need for the birthing of the *trees of life* we bring forth into our world.

Let the momma lion reveal her paws to anyone who threatens the birthing of her babies. Do not fear nor suppress your masculine energy. You have visions and dreams to birth into this life. You are a spiritual warrior of God. Your calling is high.

Love yourself first and veer not from the narrow path for no one. Your soft, nurturing heart, while very needed in our world, has been overworked and taken for granted. This is proven by the fact that the number one collective killer of women is *heart disease*.

And finally, *Keep Your Sexy Sacred.* Our world needs you to stop seeking from men what God has already given you. You already are the love you seek. You were created to share the great gifts of wisdom, understanding, and love with men so that they may evolve to the love which they too were created to be.

The woman with wisdom and understanding, no matter her looks, will always (if she so chooses) receive the gift of a loving, spiritual man who delights in her. These are the men who know that, with regard to winning the war between the flesh and the spirit, we get there to-get-*her*.

*A Woman in Harmony with her Spirit is like a river flowing.*
*She goes where she will without pretense*
*And arrives at her destination*
*Prepared to be herself and only herself*
*~Maya Angelou*

*"The Spirit and the Bride say, 'Come.' And let the one who hears say, 'Come.' And let the one who is thirsty come; let the one who desires take the water of life without price."*
*~Revelation 22:17 ESV*

# About the Author

Sabrina Universal Lawton is an extraordinary force for God in our world. She stands firmly on the principle that in order for people and organizations to evolve, love must be the driving force behind their actions. Sabrina is well known for helping seekers to embody the image and likeness of God, through her private divine appointments, retreats, books, and other products and services. The success of her Spiritual Advising Organization Evolve To Love has changed the face of therapy.

Despite a very limited formal education, prior to founding her organization, Sabrina enjoyed a lucrative sixteen-year leadership career working for various high-profile Human Capital Corporations. She was a highly-sought-after leader in the workforce, and considers her ability to lead with love to be the highest contributing factor to her success.

While Sabrina's public life was proving successful, her private life was quite challenging. In a deep moment of surrender, Sabrina had an intimate conversation with God and her true calling was spoken into her spirit. She immediately ended her corporate career to answer the call to raise the Spiritual IQ of Humanity by providing a new and way of understanding God, sex, ourselves, and one another. Sabrina has been a featured Trinity Broadcasting Network television host and looks forward to sharing God's Universal Laws of Love during Key Note Conversations around the world.

Sabrina is also the author of *Each Day a Gift*, A 90-day devotional designed to help you make a habit of giving God praise and thanks in your victories and your storms. She enjoys the gifts of God each day in the Sunshine State of Florida with her loving family.

# References

Andrew Downie. (2008) On a Remote Path to Cures.
(Ayahuasca)
https://www.nytimes.com/2008/01/01/business/worldbusines
s/01hunter.html

Anna Breslaw, Marina Khidekel, and Michelle Ruiz. (2015)
Cosmo Survey: Straight Single Women Have the Fewest
Orgasms. https://www.cosmopolitan.com/sex-
love/news/a37812/cosmo-orgasm-survey/

Author, Phil McGraw. (2003) Self Matters: Creating Your Life
from the Inside Out.
http://www.drphilstore.com/selfmatters2.html

Claudia Parker. (2018) Sabrina Universal Lawton Interview. "A
Spiritual Journey from Lust to Love." Wonder of Women.
WonderNews.
https://www.thewonderofwomen.org/wondernews/author/Cl
audia-Parker

Clergy Abuse Hotline: Shapiro, Josh. Attorney General. PA.
Criminal Prosecutions Section 888.538.8541.
https://www.attorneygeneral.gov/taking-action/press-
releases/attorney-general-shapiro-charges-catholic-priest-in-
erie-diocese-with-sexual-abuse-of-two-boys/

Dr. Sanjay Gupta, (2013) WEED: A CNN Special Report
https://www.cnn.com/2018/04/24/health/medical-marijuana-
opioid-epidemic-sanjay-gupta/index.html

Dr. Timothy Owens Moore. Author, The Science of Melanin:
Dispelling the Myths. https://www.drtmoore.com/

Gerard Powell, Rythmia Life Advancement Center (Plant
Medicine) https://www.rythmia.com/

GOVERNING. United States Marijuana Laws in 2018 Map. http://www.governing.com/gov-data/state-marijuana-laws-map-medical-recreational.html

International Center for Ethnobotanical Education Research & Service. Ayahuasca Scientific Information. http://iceers.org/science-interest-ayahuasca.php?lang=en#.W7bSPxNKgg6

Jaime Dunaway (2018) Diocese of Little Rock says 12 priests who served in state accused of sexual abuse. https://www.arkansasonline.com/news/2018/sep/10/diocese-little-rock-releases-list-12-clergy-accuse/

Leading Causes of Death (LCOD) in Females United States, 2015. https://www.cdc.gov/women/lcod/2015/index.htm

Lydia Carlis. Eyemagination Imaging. Book Cover Photo Credit. http://www.eyemaginationimaging.com

Massachusetts Institute of Technology. (2014) Eumelanin's secrets: Discovery of melanin structure may lead to better sun protection. https://www.sciencedaily.com/releases/2014/05/140522115754.htm

Michael Castleman M.A (2009) Psychology Today. The Most Important Sexual Statistic. https://www.psychologytoday.com/us/blog/all-about-sex/200903/the-most-important-sexual-statistic

News about Roman Catholic Church Sex Abuse Cases, including commentary and archival articles published in The New York Times. (2018) https://www.nytimes.com/topic/organization/roman-catholic-church-sex-abuse-cases

Pamela Madsen. (2015) 12 Crazy Amazing Facts About The Clitoris. https://www.huffingtonpost.com/pamela-madsen/12-crazy-amazing-facts-about-the-clitoris_b_7501188.html

Shaan Khan. (2016) What's Really Behind India's Rape Crisis.
https://www.thedailybeast.com/whats-really-behind-indias-rape-crisis

Statista. Global Pharmaceutical Industry - Statistics & Facts.
https://www.statista.com/topics/1764/global-pharmaceutical-industry/

Talbott Recovery. 2018 Prescription Drug Abuse Statistics You Need To Know. https://talbottcampus.com/prescription-drug-abuse-statistics/

Terence Newton, *Staff Writer (2014) IBOGA – Sacred Healing Root of Africa.*
*https://www.wakingtimes.com/2014/06/02/iboga-sacred-healing-root-africa/*

U.S. DEPARTMENT OF STATE PUBLICATION OFFICE OF THE UNDER SECRETARY FOR CIVILIAN SECURITY, DMOCRACY, AND HUMAN RIGHTS. Designed and Printed by A/GIS/GPS, TRAFFICKING IN PERSONS REPORT (2017)
https://www.state.gov/documents/organization/271339.pdf

U.S. National Child Trafficking Hotline: 888. 373.7888
https://humantraffickinghotline.org/

Vidhi Doshi (2018) Nun vs. bishop — Rape accusation rocks India's Catholic Church. The Washington Post.
https://www.washingtonpost.com/world/2018/09/14/nun-vs-bishop-rape-scandal-rocks-indias-catholic-church/?utm_term=.c91efbfa4d73

WMCActionNews5.com Staff (2018) 12 Catholic priests from AR names in sex abuse allegations.
http://www.wmcactionnews5.com/2018/09/11/catholic-priests-ar-names-sex-abuse-allegations/

Zappy Zapolin, The Reality of Truth Film (Ayahuasca) Documentary. https://youtu.be/nbsR9XqPVx0

# Free Gift for My Readers

Thank you for your wise decision to partake of this spiritual food. As a show of my universal gratitude, I am offering you a free gift to help you *win the war between the flesh and the spirit* now.

Download your 7 Keys to KYSS at www.sabrinalawton.com.

Made in the
USA
Lexington, KY